ENERGY ETHICS: A CHRISTIAN RESPONSE

Dieter T. Hessel, Editor

New York: Friendship Press

Acknowledgments

"Man-Made Radiation Hazards, U.S.A." *Women Strike for Peace.* Used by permission. "Other Ways to Go: Solar, Photovoltaic Cells, Wind, Biomass," from *Sojourners* 7, no. 6 (1978). *Sojourners*, 1309 L Street N.W., Washington, D.C. 20005. Used by permission. "Personal Conservation Guide" from *Energy: The Case for Conservation* by Denis Hayes (Washington, D.C., Worldwatch Institute, 1976). Used by permission. "Vulnerable Points of the Nuclear Fuel Cycle," from the article, "Hazards of the Nuclear Fuel Cycle," by John P. Holdren, *The Bulletin of the Atomic Scientists* 30, no. 8 (1974). Reprinted by permission of *The Bulletin of the Atomic Scientists*. © by the Educational Foundation for Nuclear Science, Chicago, Ill.

All Bible quotations are from the Revised Standard Version of the Bible, copyrighted 1946, 1952, © 1971, 1973.

Library of Congress Cataloging in Publication Data
Main entry under title:

Energy ethics, a Christian response.

   Outgrowth of a seminar of the Energy Study Panel of
the National Council of Churches of Christ in the
U.S.A. held at Abiquiu, N. M., summer 1978.
   Bibliography: p. 156
   1. Power resources—United States—Moral and
religious aspects. 2. Energy policy—United States—
Moral and religious aspects. I. Hessel, Dieter T.
II. National Council of the Churches of Christ in the
United States of America. Energy Study Panel.
TJ163.25.U6E476   261.8′5   79-19345
ISBN 0-377-00095-7

CONTENTS

To friends in the Witherspoon Society and ecumenical associations, who share a commitment to the church's social engagement as they work for change both outside and inside the energy establishment.

PREFACE

Little of the voluminous writing on the energy crunch illumines the underlying ethical questions. Scholars and journalists alike seem to be preoccupied with one question: how soon do we run out of what? This defines the problem as short supply and the solution as increased production, either by finding more of the same energy supplies (*Voilà!* There is more oil in Mexico), or by developing alternate energy technologies, some of which are very risky and costly, and therefore inappropriate.

Conservationists and proponents of a transition to a benign energy path have already challenged a one-dimensional definition of the energy problem. They have helped us to see that energy technologies, far from being morally neutral, are socially dynamic and morally consequential. Energy policy decisions affect and reflect the culture. Seemingly technical matters that could quickly tax our attention span turn out to overlay a set of profound ethical issues that require our response. Present and future inhabitants of the globe have an increasingly large stake in such questions as how energy policy is decided, what energy is produced, how it is used, and who bears the costs.

The chapters that follow grew out of the deliberations of the Energy Study Panel of the National Council of Churches of Christ in the U.S.A. Individuals on that panel worked with the editor (also on the panel) in an unusual process. Each author wrote a chapter consistent with an overall outline for this study/action book. The authors, with one exception, attended a week-long seminar at Ghost Ranch, Abiquiu, New Mexico, where each chapter was the focus for a day's discussion by a group of interested Christians, including executives from energy corporations. The authors revised their chapters in light of the seminar. In turn, the seven chapters focus on energy and religion, energy and society, energy and morality, energy and politics, energy and citizen involvement, energy and human environment, energy and the church. None of the authors is bound by the limits of his or her focus; each sees and draws connections, as we hope do readers. None of the authors is expert on particular energy technologies; each exemplifies the realization that energy policy questions cannot be left to an elite of experts. The alternative is for citizens generally, and Christians particularly, to become more alert to the key issues and more adept participants in efforts to resolve them humanely. That kind of expertise is cultivated in this book.

Energy is a study/action theme of the denominations that participate in Doing the Word (one of the Shared Approaches to Christian Education) and of the National and World Council of Churches. The values held in common by these groups call for *sufficient, sustainable energy systems for all.* This book explores these values in depth, and suggests ways to make them operational. It also fosters an action/reflection method of education that begins by clarifying our value commitments and consistent ethical criteria, analyzes various dimensions of energy policy, proposes specific action goals and methods, and reflects throughout the process on the meaning of the energy crunch.

Author Acknowledgments
I am grateful to the authors for contributing extra time and energy to this project; to James Hall, Ghost Ranch director, for sponsoring the Energy Ethics seminar; to Chris Cowap, NCC staff, for taking that opportunity for dialogue about the NCC study document; to Katherine Seelman, NCC energy consultant, for raising many of the most challenging issues in her early drafts of the Study Document; to my secretary, Neena Mitchell, for helpful editorial suggestions and bibliographical work, as well as for typing the manuscript; and to my recently enlarged family, for supporting an investment of "leisure" time to complete this project.

D.T.H.

Chapter 1:

Eco-Justice in the Eighties

*by Dieter T. Hessel**

Can we live with/without more energy? Do we confront a Malthusian dilemma of accelerating demand and limited resources? Was the energy crisis that began with the Arab oil embargo a temporary problem that the media exaggerated, or is it a watershed event in American history, with profound religious, moral, social, economic, and political implications?

Five years after the oil embargo, the energy news seemed almost upbeat. Except for minor disruptions, adequate oil was being produced and per capita use of oil and gas had decreased modestly. More oil had been found in Mexico and more nuclear power plants were being constructed, despite growing citizen protest. More workers in the energy industry were making record wages. Congress had finally passed a national energy act. Why get excited about an empty energy tub, or that fateful crossover point when the demand line on the graph exceeds supply? All that "establishment dire" about possibly freezing in the eighties seemed overstated, before 1979.

Suddenly, the Iranian Revolution reduced U.S. oil imports 10 percent, triggered another price rise by OPEC, posed the need for

*Associate for Social Education, Program Agency, United Presbyterian Church, U.S.A., New York City.

1

mandatory conservation, and underscored the long lead time needed to deliver alternative fuels. Meanwhile, the ominous, partial meltdown of the nuclear reactor at Three Mile Island aroused mass anxiety and vigorous public debate over appropriate energy technologies. On top of that President Carter announced decontrol of domestically produced oil, and called for a tax on some of the oil companies' windfall profits. Little was said about ways to protect poor, fixed- and middle-income Americans from the severe effects of soaring petroleum prices and rising utility rates. All of which threw energy questions back into the lap of Congress, which in 1978 avoided the tough issues and failed to pass an effective, fair national energy policy.

The postpetroleum, postnuclear era has begun; there is time to make an orderly transition to alternative energy systems that are socially just and environmentally safe. The energy crunch, someone has said, is "the outward and visible sign of an inward, invisible chaos." Misplaced values and concentrated economic power have fostered energy-intensive systems of production/consumption, and heightened public anxiety about the scarcity of fossil fuels. The focus now shifts to the design (both what and how) of a better future. Many people view the energy crisis as an opportunity to shift to more community-based, decentralized energy sources, involving small business, job creation, and appropriate economic development. All levels of government, however, have been slow to respond. Given the heavy social and human costs of high energy development, and the major lifestyle changes required by light energy systems, what should be the emphasis for mobilization?

The Current Social Situation

Consider how urgent is the need to envision an energy future that is not the energy past writ large. G.K. Chesterton once bemoaned "a flat wilderness of standardization" where people are chained to "enlargement without liberty and progress without hope." He was referring to the effects of bolshevism or big business, but his would be an apt comment on the response to the energy crunch of powerful, or power-seeking, nations. Energy is the ability to do work and to move objects. Energy promises military and economic power; many governments and people want as much, as soon, as possible. But with what results?

Developed societies like the US have reached a stage of exhaustive energy strength. The policy required heavy investment in ever larger, more complex and centralized energy forms to do whatever might be asked. "The result was a rather expensive array of trip hammers capable of cracking any conceivable nut." The alternative, emphasizes Amory Lovins, is "to meet different [energy] needs with an elegant frugality of energy supplied in the most effective and appropriate way for each particular task."[1] Elegant frugality of energy suggests diverse, renewable, relatively simple systems scaled to end-use. It would mean less generation of electricity, which is both economically and environmentally expensive. Electricity would be reserved for premium uses, not for low-grade heating and cooling.

But will we change our lifestyles accordingly? Energy policy is a subject freighted with clashing images and expectations. When asked about the energy situation, producers and politicians usually look somber. They invoke a major responsibility to maintain our high standard of living and to preserve, in perpetuity, civilization as we know it. They assume that the more energy we use, the better off we are; to be even better off, we need even more energy. The energy producers go on to claim the technical know-how and a public mandate to solve the energy problem by rapid exploration and extraction of minerals, reduced regulation and increased tax credits, subsidy for development of synthetic fuels, and relaxed environmental safeguards.[2] Energy producers tend to be short-tempered about voluntary groups of critical or visionary citizens "who don't know what they are doing, or what we need to do the job." This assumes that the "job" is to increase supply rapidly in already projected ways. The energy establishment in business and government sees a limited role for citizens as supporters of prevailing policy and as responsible consumers who are unlikely to reduce consumption significantly.

Suppose, however, that people want to consume less energy and to participate in shaping a society that has sufficient, sustainable energy systems for all. People with this view need to reexamine what kind of energy future is planned by whom, for whom. They will want to explore viable alternatives, for they sense that humane surroundings, social equality, environmental safety, and civil liberties are affected by what first looked like a mere question of supply. They discern that the energy problem is much more complex than the modern equivalent of gathering wood. Energy policy shapes the whole social system, and reinforces particular cultural values. In fact, energy paths differ primarily in their social goals, and the means planned to reach the goals. Those who view more energy as better would elevate a means to an end. Those who view more energy consumption as a measure of failure are asserting that social goals should control energy methods.

Demand for energy is usually perceived in relation to economic growth, productivity, employment, and US power in the world. But the economic growth pattern should be evaluated in terms of its overall contribution to the general welfare. Economist Herman E. Daly examines two couplings relating energy to its *raison d'être*, welfare:

Energy → GNP → General Welfare

> Both of these couplings are assumed to be tight in most energy demand projections, when in fact they are loose. The looseness of the energy→GNP coupling has been shown by the Ford Energy Policy Project study which estimates that energy growth rates could be cut in half with hardly any effect on GNP growth rate. . . . Sweden and West Germany have half the per capita energy consumption of the US, and yet the Swedes and Germans live about as well, perhaps better, than Americans. The second coupling, GNP→General Welfare, is increasingly recognized as loose . . . a growing minority (of economists) doubt the net welfare benefits of more GNP. Thus the easy equation of "more energy equals greater welfare" breaks down at two points. As the looseness of these two couplings becomes more widely realized, the energy projections based on their presumed tightness will be shown to have been exaggerated.[3]

In fact, nothing is binding about the future demand curves that appear in most books on energy. They can become self-undoing, rather than self-fulfilling prophecies.

Citizen Responsibility

To understand the dynamics and details of the energy debate takes homework plus a willingness to probe behind official reports, press releases, and media education programs. Since no source of information gives the whole story, there is no substitute for exploring various sources of information and soliciting the views of independent students of energy issues, victims of existing energy policy, organizers of alternative energy groups, as well as energy producers and regulators.[4]

More and more citizens' groups are stepping out of supportive roles onto center stage. Not only are they serious about energy conservation; they also want to do their own assessment of energy policy choices and to help make better choices on the basis of sound values and data. This book is designed to foster such initiative.

Now that we discern that energy policy issues are at least as social-political-economic as they are technical, there are no experts to defer to. Only specialists, special interests, public interest groups, and people with special needs. No elite of producers, researchers, or public officials has the right or the ability to decide such a far-reaching question as: what kind of energy do we need, produced how, for what purposes, to whose benefit, at what cost to whom? The potential controversy built into each clause of that question is sobering indeed.

So we must become serious about analyzing and acting on energy issues, but not so serious as to lose our sense of humor. An alternative energy movement has arisen in the land. Color it green, not red. It protests toxic technologies fostered by ultracapitalist enterprises. (Which is more "radical," the green movement or the energy establishment?) Its methods are peacefully democratic and coalitional, disciplined and demonstrative. Its genre is funny T-shirts and cartoons and songs such as those published by the Clamshell Alliance, whose musicians would agree with the words on Woody Guthrie's guitar case, "This machine kills Fascists."

Humor needs to season the movement toward reduced consumption of energy. Notice the artful method of two writers, Bruce M. Hannon and Timothy G. Lohman, in *The American Journal of Public Health*:

> We have calculated the total fossil energy equivalent of the food calories [that could be] saved by reducing the present degree of overweight (2.3 billion pounds for the adult United States population) to optimum body weight. . . . The energy saved [would be] equivalent to 1.3 billion gallons of gasoline, and the annual energy saving [from] the energy required to plant, harvest, feed, transport, wholesale, retail, acquire, store, and cook the required food . . . would more than supply the annual residential electrical demands of Boston, Chicago, San Francisco, and Washington, D.C.

Lifestyle change need not be grim business. Christians, at least, ought to celebrate the Community of the New Age as they seek "abundant" life in a world with limited resources, and as they act to change lifestyles in ways that serve distributive justice. Church programs that focus immediately on how to reduce consumption hardly do enough theologically and politically; and they may even do too much by focusing singularly on doing without. Those who would be more-conserving-than-thou reflect a formidable Pharisaism which contradicts the ethic of Jesus—his teaching and celebration of the abundant life. Jesus pointed to the abundance of fully-restored relationships, freedom to enjoy community, and power to exhibit the Kingdom of God here and now.

The power of the Kingdom of God, exhibited in simplicity, sharing and solidarity, is subversive of the dominant American cult of power. Our culture's prevailing "monomyth" features the extraordinary power of superheroes who are available to save a passive public from evil or disaster.[5] The large energy corporations appear to welcome an opportunity to play superhero, protecting against "sinister" alien mineral cartels and rooting out machine-destroying Luddites. (The American myth does not anticipate that a superhero might be dangerous too.)

Christians, however, are disciples of a nonsuperhero, who refuses to turn stones into bread even while pointing to the limits of principalities and powers. The Christian story clashes sharply with the American cult of energy. The Christian story points to a fulfilling context of meaning and a spirit of living that would be negated by more and more energy consumption, violent technology, and hoarding of possessions.

The connection between reduced consumption and enriched community deserves more exploration in all aspects of daily living. The energy crunch may help to displace the conventional wisdom that "more is better," with the new insight that "less of the same" may halt progressive impoverishment and could enhance quality of life.

"More is better" would accelerate the disintegrating effects of *over*development. Overdevelopment means that the food we eat, the air we breathe, the water we drink, the cities and office buildings we inhabit, the enterprises from which we profit, the products we consume, the lives we lead, are contaminating our whole selves, body and spirit, in ways we have yet to understand. An overdeveloped society piles up products, missiles, energy, but it creates deep pockets of poverty as well as high levels of unemployment. Overdevelopment relies on, even increases, underdevelopment wherein 85 percent of the world's resources is used for the benefit of less than 20 percent of the world's population.

In the mid-1970s the United States, with 6 percent of the world's population, was using a third of the world's oil production, nearly two-thirds of the natural gas, and over one-fifth of the coal. The United States is to energy consumption what Saudi Arabia is to production—the single overwhelming factor.

> In 1975, Americans *wasted* more fossil fuel than was used by two-thirds of the world's population. . . . Energy is "wasted" whenever work is performed that could have been completed with less or lower quality energy without incurring higher total

social or economic costs. . . . Major areas in which significant savings could be made are (in order of magnitude) transportation, heating and cooling systems for buildings, water heating, the food system, electrical generation, industrial efficiency, waste recovery, recycling, and lighting.[6]

Conservation is no longer a marginal activity, but a major facet of responsible energy policy designed to bridge the next two decades without becoming hooked on dangerous or unreliable technologies. All of which points to a new social norm.

Sufficiency as a Norm

A broad movement toward energy sufficiency would significantly alter American life. William E. Gibson has developed the sufficiency principle as a positive standard for evaluating social progress. Social health is measured in terms of meeting human need rather than in terms of production achieved and goods acquired. Sufficiency is the norm of justice; those who have more than enough aggravate insufficiency among others and themselves.

> Even though we cannot draw the line precisely at the point where sufficiency ends and excess consumption starts, a standard appropriate to the present world situation would insist that the majority of Americans consume far too much. . . . The overconsumers need a downward redefinition of their lifestyle in the direction of sufficiency. . . . What any one person may include in the idea of what is sufficient for himself or herself is necessarily limited by the ideas of others about their sufficiency and the recognition that some minimal sufficiency for everyone takes precedence over anyone's right to enjoy a surplus. . . .There can be no minimum levels of sufficiency unless we find ways to set maximums upon incomes and wealth. There is urgent need at this juncture for clarification of the policy goals that can bring minimums and maximums into operation.[7]

Public policy must limit the maximum energy available for any one use or user, and plan to meet at affordable prices the minimum energy needs of all. Sufficiency for all becomes both the goal and the means of a just energy policy. The norm displaces the notion that there is never sufficient energy. Sufficiency indicates ceilings and floors, but in a flexible, creative way. Efficient energy use becomes socially important, as does each method of achieving efficiency. Adequate insulation of existing housing, for example, would save

more energy and create more employment at less cost than would all
the projected nuclear power development. Moreover, energy sufficiency derives from public participation—communities of people
planning together how best to produce and use energy for the
common good.

Many people seem prepared to forego the additional energy needed
for luxurious living, and want to avoid the effects of toxic energy
technologies, in exchange for healthy, humane living conditions.
They want to participate in planning for sufficient energy use and
sustainable energy technologies. Energy *sufficiency* requires stringent
conservation, more equitable allocation of available energy, technologies appropriate to and planned by local communities, and lifestyles
of sharing. *Sustainable* energy systems would limit ecological risks
and impacts.

All energy technologies involve some risk, but further development
of toxic technologies, such as extensive burning of coal or operation
of nuclear power plants, can create severe, irreversible conditions of
catastrophe. "In the case of technologies that threaten the possibility
of irreversible global damage, a major ethical question is whether it
is fair for present generations to reap the benefits while future
generations bear the cost."[8] Preferable energy technologies are those
that present less severe and less involuntary risks.

Eco-Justice in Biblical Perspective[9]

The norms of sufficiency and sustainability are integrally related,
even causally connected. To put it another way, justice to the deprived
and care for nature are two sides of the same ethic of eco-justice.
This ethic, which informs all chapters of this book and is given
detailed attention in chapters 4 and 7, is characteristic of biblical
faith. The striking biblical insight is that injustice leads to chaos, both
socially and environmentally. What people do and how nature acts
are interrelated. Micah 3:9-12 is a good example. "Hear this, you
heads of the house of Jacob. . .who abhor justice and pervert all
equity, who build Zion with blood and Jerusalem with
wrong. . . . Zion shall be plowed as a field; Jerusalem shall become a
heap of ruins, and the mountain of the house a wooded height."
Social injustice has profound environmental consequences. Economic
and energy policies that would be environmentally safe must be
socially fair. Otherwise both humans and nature suffer catastrophe.

Biblical thought does not idolize nature, but it recognizes that
human existence is close to nature, that human beings are limited
creatures.

1. *Life for humankind can only be right in covenant with the God who entrusts the planet to human care.* Commenting on Genesis 1:26-28, John Calvin wrote: "Man was already created in this condition, that the earth was subject to him; but he enjoys it only when he understands that it has been leased to him by the Lord. It is true, as common sense tells us, that all the goods of the world are naturally intended for our use. But as Lordship over the world has been taken away from us in Adam, all the gifts of God we touch are polluted by our sin. . . ."

2. *The material benefits of creation and human endeavor are a gift of God for the whole human race.* Human beings are called to be *stewards*, rather than *owners*, of material resources and products of human endeavor. (Stewardship, biblically understood, is communal, ecological, and intergenerational.) The image of the steward in the New Testament empowers and encourages just economic activity, while it qualifies every right to property or exercise of power. The *oikonomos* or house manager is responsible for the well-being of the *oikos*, the dwelling and all its inhabitants. All the inhabitants in the *oikos* include people, livestock, land, resources, and the industry and commerce derived therefrom. Human beings are responsible for a complex web of biological, cultural, and political systems. In Jesus' teaching, "The steward was at any moment accountable, not primarily for the profits he earned for his master, but for the faithfulness of his dealings with the servants as well as with the goods (Luke 12:41 ff.). This steward image was broadened by Paul to apply to the whole calling of the Christian—'servants of Christ and stewards of the mysteries of God' (I Cor. 4:1), but the material dimension was not lost from it."[10] In God's plan (*oikonomia*), economic activity, including energy production and use, is intended to be part of the harmony of the whole.

3. *The purpose of economic activity and energy systems is to serve human need.* The faithful and wise steward of Luke 12 acts according to the master's will. "Everyone to whom much is given, of him will much be required; and of him to whom men commit much will they demand the more." In the parable of the vineyard (Matt. 21:33 ff.), those tenants who "kill" the son and try to seize the property are punished, and the vineyard is let out to other tenants. Modern enterprises that violate the *oikos* and foster uncaring patterns of resource use incur costs and "punishments" that may indeed threaten our tenancy.

4. *The needs of the poor have priority over the comfort of the rich.* Scarce resources must be distributed equitably. This is the main thrust

of biblical teaching about justice—not to everyone his or her due, but
to each according to need (cf. Acts 4:34 ff., Exod. 22:25, Isa. 55:1,
Luke 6:20-21). The poor at home and abroad are the touchstone of
policy; their needs deserve special consideration. Unless the people at
the bottom are protected, there can be no better future. Property is
rightly possessed when it is justly used. Personal property must not
be sought at the expense of others. Harvesters should leave some of
the crops for the poor (Lev. 19:9-10). The Prophets are quick to
condemn those who exploit the weak (Isa. 3:14-15, Ezek. 18:10-13,
Amos 2:6-7). Jesus' teachings go further, as in his encounter with the
rich young ruler (Matt. 19:16-24). It is apparent that inequitable
distribution of scarce energy resources cannot be squared with biblical
principles. Nor can it be just that the poor pay high prices or do
without basic energy products, while the rich pursue enjoyment of
luxuries.

5. *Human beings are accountable to future generations as well as to
those who are now alive.* We are responsible for actual conditions that
future persons will encounter. Neither serious evil nor responsibility
to combat it has a time limit. Motivation to think beyond the needs
of our own group and generation stems from Christian faith in the
providence of God. The Creator, Governor and Redeemer has
purposes that include us, but extend far beyond us. In response to
God's love, we are enabled to love near and distant neighbors, both
our contemporaries and generations unborn. In the covenant, God
promises blessing "to you and to your descendants forever" (Gen.
13:15, 28:13-14, Exod. 33:1). We are obligated to protect for future
generations the resources given to us by the processes of geology and
our human predecessors.[11] We who inherit a good land must preserve
and enhance it (cf. Deut. 6:10-11). A similar sense of continuity
prevails in the communion of saints who are bound together in the
historical sweep of God's reconciling action.

But the claims of present and future generations seem to clash, as
we face critical problems of world poverty, resource limits, and
exploding prices. How much emphasis should be placed on sustaining
today's living versus planning for greater numbers in the future? The
biblical emphasis is clear.

6. *Concern for the future cannot allow us to dilute or withhold our
care for those who live now, especially "the least" or the wretched of
the earth.* We do not have the right to choose who lives and who dies
in order to serve current economic ideologies or some projected
posterity. We have no right to squander the world's energy resources

for wasteful and ostentatiously affluent short-term self-benefit. We have no right to ignore basic needs of deprived people living now or to disregard the health of generations yet to be born.

7. *Reductions in energy production and consumption should be evaluated in eschatological perspective, i.e., in view of where history is going.* Sacrifices of energy are not necessarily losses, in light of the Kingdom of God, which, though not yet, is already here, and which promises blessing to those who relinquish power and serve others. The eschatological visions of the Bible portray a peaceful world of people, with claims and needs satisfied, living amiably in the community of creation and in communion with the Creator (Isa. 11:6-9, Hosea 2:18-23, Rev. 21:2-4).

God's restorative purpose for a violated world is to reunite all things. Our choice is to wait for the denouement to happen apocalyptically, or to help effect partial restoration here and now. The first choice means resigning to fate; the alternative is a response of faith, faith in the One who creates, governs, and redeems existence and invites responsive acts of creativity, cultivation, and restoration.

Pertinent Ethical Criteria

Eco-justice, as biblically understood, does not produce detailed blueprints for dealing with the energy situation. There is no direct line from the Bible to social policy. But social policy guidelines can be more or less consistent with the eco-justice ethic. The energy policy implications of eco-justice are suggested in a *preliminary* way in the following selected list of social impact criteria:[12]

1. Energy decisions should be made on the basis of direct and adequately funded citizen participation, with access to all relevant data from public and private sources, while limiting the undue ability of any particular group to influence public opinion. Energy policy should provide for meaningful public participation in decision-making by those who are affected.

2. Users of energy should, as far as possible, bear its full costs. Decisions should not place one group at risk for the benefit of an entirely different group.

3. The policy of each political unit should be to strive toward energy self-sufficiency.

4. Energy systems are preferable that are small and understandable enough to lend themselves to informed participatory decision-making at the lower levels of the political process.

5. Because the possibilities of energy growth are limited, energy

should be used primarily to meet essential human needs, even if this requires fundamental changes in the global concepts and patterns of economic growth and development.

6. An energy policy which critically disrupts and/or renders useless the land and results in the disruption of the culture, the families, and the lives of the people on the land is unacceptable.

7. An energy policy that discriminates against the poor, individual and societal rights, religious, occupational, ethnic subgroups, and future generations is unacceptable.

8. The development of a full range of decentralized, benign and renewable energy systems should be encouraged and supported to enable people to have the freedom to choose their energy systems.

9. The protection of the long-run health and evolutionary potential of the biosphere should override all short-term economic considerations in developing energy policies.

10. Energy technologies should not concentrate power over the natural environment into the hands of a few.

11. Energy systems which minimize the use of depletable resources are to be preferred.

12. The establishment of health and safety standards should not demand absolute proof or absolute certainty of risk; in matters of uncertainty, decisions should be made in favor of protecting life and health.

13. When a decision is made which necessarily entails loss of life, there must be compelling reasons for taking the risk, and the persons whose lives are involved must have a way of avoiding the risk.

14. Energy decisions must be based on the long-term need for providing meaningful work (valued as a process and a product by both worker and society) for the un- and underemployed as well as the fully employed.

15. The human costs and benefits of employment changes caused by energy shifts must be shared equitably throughout society.

In this introductory chapter, space does not permit a lengthy discussion of how these ethical criteria come to bear on particular energy policy choices. Two illustrations must suffice, one having to do with nuclear wastes, the other with the poor and unemployed.

Nuclear power is already in trouble on economic grounds; investors no longer perceive a promising future in nuclear power. But even if it be an economic and technological brontosaurus, it will leave us with a large deposit of perpetually *hot* bones. By the year 2000, in the United States alone, there will be dozens of useless "decommissioned" reactors that remain permanently hazardous, thousands of tons of high-level radioactive wastes produced by weapons manufacture and electric utilities, a similar quantity of tailings from uranium mining and milling, and one billion cubic feet of low-level radioactive garbage—tools, equipment, clothing, fluids—that remains toxic for "only" two to three hundred years and would cover the entire length of Interstate 80, one foot deep. The waste has been managed haphazardly to date.

The energy establishment's reassurances about the nuclear waste problem are of theological-ethical interest. As the late Rep. Leo J. Ryan (Democrat, California) observed during 1977 congressional hearings, "The management of these wastes seems to have been virtually dismissed with an attitude that American technology will take care of it when the time comes." Precisely that attitude was expressed by Robert J. Gileson, chairman of the board of Philadelphia Electric Company, in comments to the *Philadelphia Inquirer*, November 23, 1978: "As a nation we've gotten so doggone self-conscious about solving the problems before we do anything. . . . To ask the power plants of this country to [find] a no-waste solution is like saying to the auto industry at the turn of the century, 'You must solve the whole problem of air pollution.' We know we're going to create a problem, but you have to have confidence in the future."

The ethical rejoinder must focus on criteria numbers 8, 9, 10, 12, and 13. Responsibility requires the avoidance of ecologically hazardous processes and products. Previously, industrial society placed the burden of proof on those who questioned the advisability of public and private undertakings made possible by new technological expertise. It is time to shift the burden upon those who advocate potentially risky techniques, processes and projects, to show how any proposed venture would cooperate with "the natural." In addition, energy producers should be accountable to the residents of communities where their facilities are located.

One must also note the false optimism about technology on the part of the utility executive. His belief that something will turn up is not to be confused with Christian hope, which knows that the better future that God brings can override the existing order and will bring judgment on the way to peace.

Meanwhile, to take up our second illustration of an ethically conscious approach to energy policy, what about the poor and the unemployed? Are their actual immediate needs being traded off in order to meet probable future needs of the unborn? "Black people and poor people have seen their fuel costs rise, their jobs endangered, and their interests ignored," warns Vernon Jordan. He advocates *conservation* programs that involve assistance to the poor, and development of *renewable* resources utilizing sun, wind, water, and nonconventional technologies, such as cogeneration, using industrial byproducts. Renewable resources offer employment potential and consumer benefits. "The third pillar of sound national energy strategy has to be *assistance to poor people*." In particular this requires effective measures to shield the poor from the effects of high energy prices and shortages, through lifeline utility rates, subsidized programs of insulation, and energy stamps.[13]

In the energy field, eco-justice coalitions must be built, coalitions that will advocate the needs of both those who are deprived today and those who will be deprived tomorrow. (Refer to criteria numbers 2, 4, 7, 8, 14, 15.) Such coalitions will grasp their responsibility to *near and distant neighbors*, bridging class, geography, time. They will discern that indifference to the poor today will make many more poor tomorrow, because unjust distribution of resources and concentrations of power, if unchallenged, worsen faster than they can be ameliorated by compensatory gestures.

Conclusion

Social justice and environmental health occur together or not at all. Readers of this book share responsibility, with others of good will, to work creatively for sufficient, sustaining energy for all.

Failure to assert these norms and to make them operational in American politics can only leave us more dependent on large energy enterprises that acquire and sell minerals or generate electricity for profit. Eco-justice, however, gives priority to the common good—in light of the goodness of God—and depends on the responsible action of the citizenry.

In response to issues of energy policy, church bodies, leaders, and members must continue the ecumenical quest for "a just, participatory, and sustainable society" that came into focus at the 1975 Assembly of the World Council of Churches in Nairobi. In a major address to that assembly, Australian biologist Charles Birch warned:

> We know how to use science and technology to produce a
> rich society but not how to produce a just one. The rich must
> live more simply that the poor may simply live.
>   . . .[Given an unjust world] it is now totally unintelligible for
> the churches to operate as though there is one plane called the

spiritual which is their area and another called the temporal which they can leave to others. This leads to the false belief that all they have to do is to change people and that changed people will change the world. It has not worked out that way. The redemption of people involves the redemption of the world they live in. The struggle for liberation is a struggle against those bonds that confine people all over the world, economically, politically, and technically as well as spiritually. It is vital for the churches to be involved in all these tasks and to question seriously their commitment to the technically dominated society. . . .

If we are to break the poverty barrier for almost two-thirds of the earth's people, if we are to continue to inhabit the earth, there has to be a revolution in the relationship of human beings to the earth and of human beings to each other. The churches of the world have now to choose whether or not they become part of that revolution.

Chapter 2:

Energy and Society: Choosing a Future

*by Scott Paradise**

Social History and Energy Systems

Only three times in the long march of history has society devised a fundamentally new energy system. For its first million years the human race, as it gradually emerged from the mists of the past, lived as hunters and gatherers. Hunter-gatherers use the power of their own muscles to reap the stored energy in plants and animals through unmanipulated natural processes. They adjust to the biological energy system of their environment. Since the energy in nature rarely concentrates in a single neighborhood for long and fluctuates with seasons, hunter-gatherer populations tend to be small, scattered and somewhat migratory. Because of their size, hunter-gatherer societies have remained the original classless society. They require only the simplest of governments because of their dispersion. They can, because of their need to carry their possessions when they migrate, accumulate little wealth. But life for hunter-gatherers, far from being nasty, brutish, and short, has often afforded both the necessities of life and the leisure to develop complex cultures. Most all human experience has been lived in this kind of society. Until the invention of agriculture, there was no other.[1]

---
*Episcopal Chaplain, Massachusetts Institute of Technology, Cambridge, Massachusetts.

16

The Invention of Agriculture

The emergence of agriculture ten thousand years ago constitutes the first great transformation in the condition of human life. It coincided with the development of the first solar energy system. The planting, harvesting and storage of crops made possible settled populations of greater size and greater concentration. This in turn made possible the beginning of architecture and the accumulation of wealth. For thousands of years, however, first in the Middle East, then in the Orient, Africa and the Americas, the diffuseness of the sun's rays made the village the largest viable size for human settlement. The life in the agricultural village has stood as the norm of human experience until the present century.[2]

The Rise of Cities

After approximately five thousand years of village agriculture, conditions which opened the way for the rise of cities and the emergence of civilization took shape in a few places. So profound were the new possibilities implicit in these changes that they mark humankind's second great transformation. Although the source of energy driving this new form of society remained the sun, irrigation and other forms of hydraulic technology made possible, and required for its full use, large populations and the concentration of political power. The trick of using a diffuse energy source like the sun in societies with concentrations of population, wealth, and political power proved so difficult to maintain that most civilizations could not survive more than a few hundred years. The rise and the fall of civilizations made up the stuff of history until modern times. Generally, as after the fall of Rome, the collapse of a civilization resulted in the reversion of society to an array of decentralized agricultural villages. Civilizations, while they could be maintained, made possible the large integrated economic, political, and institutional structures and the high culture associated with urban life. They also brought political tyranny, large-scale slavery, and increasingly destructive warfare.

The Industrial Revolution

New circumstances at the end of the Middle Ages in England served as the womb for the third great transformation. Here the improvement of agriculture, the large-scale production of iron and steel, the development of machinery, and the factory mode of production spawned the industrial revolution. But behind these changes lay a new energy system based on the fast expansion of the use of coal as fuel. Coal dominated industrial society's energy system until well into the twentieth century, when oil and gas superseded it. Without these cheap, concentrated and abundant fossil fuels the explosive growth of population, wealth, technology, production, and trade would have been impossible. In many respects, however, industrial civilizations shared characteristics of the urban civilizations of the past. Like them, industrial civilization developed large integrated economic, political, and institutional structures. Like them, it developed the forms of high urban culture. Like them, it developed highly sophisticated forms of political tyranny and oppression and highly destructive forms of warfare.

In two important ways industrial society differs strikingly from traditional civilizations. First, huge consumption of fossil fuels and employment of modern technology have made possible unprecedented production of goods and accumulation of wealth, with luxury for large numbers of people. Although this production has proven possible without the traditional forms of slavery, a large portion of humanity is left out of the productive process or benefits little from the wealth it produces.

Second, industrial society exhibits growth and innovation rates so much faster than any previous civilization that a new situation has resulted. The increase of world population is the most obvious kind of growth. It doubled in the eighty years between 1850 and 1930. It doubled again in the forty-five years between 1930 and 1975. Though growth rates have peaked, world population may double again in the thirty-five years between 1975 and 2010.[3] Meanwhile, technological innovation has accelerated so rapidly that many persons living today can remember a world in which no automobiles, airplanes, or radios existed. And some of them as children talked with people born before the development of railroads. Technological changes in transportation and communication have been viewed, until quite recently, as instruments of progress. Now that they are being reexamined for the rate of energy consumed and the quality of life delivered, further innovations may have a different character.

Innovative, energy-intensive technology exacerbates two tendencies in industrial society that it shares with traditional civilizations like Egypt and Babylonia. (1.) These civilizations developed large integrated economic and political systems. Industrial (and postindustrial) society is fast incorporating the whole world into its integrated economy. (2.) Traditional civilizations tended to be so unstable that few could flourish for more than a few hundred years. Industrial society also becomes dysfunctional as it depletes resources, pollutes the environment, and manufactures weaponry, all at a rate which many judge cannot be sustained for even a century longer.

Since this society has grown upon a foundation of cheap and abundant fossil fuels, and since the end of the age of such fuels approaches rapidly, a time for decision has come. The decision we make depends as much upon attitudes as on our technological options regarding energy.

A Psychohistory of Energy

Just as history reveals connections between the evolution of new energy systems and social transformations, so historical speculation suggests links between energy and cultural attitudes about power. The psychic lives of the earliest races evade our scrutiny. We can, however, draw inferences from what archaeologists unearth. We can draw parallels between observations of those anthropologists who study hunter-gatherer societies today and what hunter-gatherer societies must have been like before the dawn of history.[4] By so doing we can perceive another set of stages in human development.

The Pre-Promethean Experience

The first stage, by far the longest, stretches through the period before the discovery of fire. Until then people depended entirely on the energy of their own bodies. They observed with awe the great physical powers of nature. But because they lacked the means, they could not control or manipulate these powers technologically. However, assuming theirs were like the most primitive cultures known today, they made no distinction between the power in nature "out there" and their own psychic experience. They invested the natural world with spiritual power and intentions. Likewise they considered that the psychic and magical powers of the shaman were as real as any other kind. When a group of Eskimos in northern Canada was told about the moon landing, they were hardly impressed. "Our shaman has done that several times," they responded. The spiritual powers of the shamans seemed to influence people in the material world. The physical world itself seemed rife with spiritual powers which could and did influence people. Spiritual and physical power were one. The earliest people viewed them alike with fear, awe, and interest.[5]

The Desacralization Process

The discovery of fire gave people their first experience of manipulating a powerful natural force. Henceforth, by slow, almost imperceptible increments, human societies developed technologies which could give them power over their environment. With the invention of agriculture, they harnessed the sun and created the first energy system. But in spite of this achievement, the power of technology must have seemed miniscule compared to the power of the spirit world. In fact, technological power was then considered to be a branch of magic or religion. The church's blessing of the fields and formal prayers for rain and good harvests, which even today survive in places, give witness to a perspective that once was all but universal. The earlier identification of these two kinds of power stands out in political and military decisions. For example, Constantine embraced Christianity because he saw in the cross a source of power greater than and just as efficacious as a legion. Bede reports that in a battle between the Christian Welsh and invading pagan Anglo-Saxons, a rank of monks processed onto the battlefield to pray against the infidels. The invaders cut them down in order to stop their prayers.

It may have been this association of technological power with the spiritual that made the quest for increasing and wielding power both intriguing and fearful. Myths dramatize this ambivalence. Prometheus made the use of fire known to people. But in order to do so, he had to steal it from the gods and bring down upon himself their eternal punishment. Babel saw the prospect of people organizing and making bricks and achieving great things. Divine jealousy frustrated this plan. In New Testament times, according to the Gospel account, the Devil himself tempted Jesus in the wilderness with power to produce bread from stones and thus feed the world's hungry.

But in spite of this ambivalence, technology did advance, society began to wield more power, and the distinction between spiritual power and technological power began to take shape. Harvey Cox and others[6] view the biblical teaching that desacralizes nature as a foundation stone of technological society. Lynn White blames this same teaching as the cause of the environmental crisis.[7] In either case, Carl Jung maintains that "people must strip nature of psychic attributes in order to dominate it ... and the idea of baptism lifts a man out of his archaic identification with the world and changes him into a being who stands above it."[8]

Enter the Dynamo

The choice of the exact time when the next stage in the psycho-history of energy begins is arbitrary. But Henry Adams, in his *Education*, gives us a date, a symbol and a rationale.[9] In 1895, when he toured Normandy and the neighboring regions, he was deeply impressed by the beauty and power of the medieval churches and cathedrals which made every town and village in the region a jewel. He noted that almost without exception the builders dedicated these spectacular shrines to the Virgin and that the Virgin represented a source of immense and terrifying spiritual energy. He was not endorsing a literal acceptance of medieval Mariolatry, but rather noting the tremendous creative power, spiritual energy, and even biological force in the feminine principle. It was this principle, well-known in primitive societies, crystallized in the cults of Venus, Diana, and Aphrodite in pagan antiquity, that transformed the landscape of medieval France. Reflecting on his New England background, Adams added that Puritans knew that sex was sin. In any previous age, sex was strength. Goddesses were worshiped not for their beauty but because of their force. This was reproduction, the highest energy ever known to humankind, the subject of four-fifths of the noblest art, which exercises vastly more attraction over the human mind than all the steam engines ever dreamed of.

And yet North American culture knew little of her power. Sex became sentiment, not a force. Although the Virgin still had power at Lourdes, everywhere in industrial society that power seemed to be waning. It was as if another kind of power had preempted the Virgin's throne and the thrones of the other sources of spiritual power. Adams found the symbol for the newly enthroned source of power in the Hall of Dynamos at the Great Exposition in Paris in 1900. For him the forty-foot dynamo became a symbol of infinity, a moral force, much as the early Christians felt the Cross. Thus the immense growth of mechanical energy in the nineteenth century produced a cultural revolution, completing the transition begun with the discovery of fire. No longer was spiritual energy the source of all power. Instead, physical or technological power became the only energy worth talking about. Today, it is taken for granted that the energy crisis refers to the rising cost of fossil fuels rather than the fossilization of spirituality. And with the triumph of the dynamo came the end of the ambivalence toward energy that played a central role in myths of the past. Even those who relish the last vestiges of that ambivalence in science-fiction paperbacks embrace with enthusiasm a high-energy life style.

The New Situation

Since the death of Henry Adams the development of large-scale technology in the service of extensive, complex institutions has created a new situation. Never before has so much energy been available for human use. Since World War II we have used 50 percent of all the energy used in human history. Ordinary individuals in industrial societies have more horsepower at their disposal than did kings in ages past. The novelty of this sheer quantity of energy is matched by its concentrations. In this century, the governments of industrial nations have increased and centralized their power. In recent decades the appearance and expansion of multinational corporations and energy conglomerates has placed in the hands of the leaders of a few institutions the power to determine much about the future of the planet. These firms are drawing the whole world into a single integrated economy dedicated to the establishment of a universal high-energy consumer culture. No previous time has seen on a global basis such acceleration of growth and social change as that caused by these institutions.

Better living for all stands as the well-publicized promise offered by the present industrial society. And although in absolute numbers more people are hungry than ever before, it is true that today more people, and a higher percentage of people, are richer than at any time in the past. The revolution of rising expectations suggests that increasingly the world's poor believe that economic development and industrialization will bring affluence even to them.

But the costs and dangers of the present order are no less familiar.[10] The voracious appetite of the growing world economy exploits resources at an unprecedented and accelerating rate. Huge though the global reserves of usable natural resources are, present trends ensure their depletion within an ominously brief time. The processes of the world economy poison the environment on which we all depend. And the misuse of land and water threatens over time to transform large parts of the earth into desert.

The shift from a world consisting of many societies with largely self-reliant economies to a single global society with an integrated economy makes the whole system vulnerable to disaster, should one essential part of the system malfunction. The blackout caused by a small transformer accident that paralyzed the American Northeast stands as an example of what may come. War in the Middle East or large-scale revolution in southern Africa could cut off oil and mineral supplies essential for America's economic functioning. Thus while the global economy serves us, it also makes us dependent, transforming us into its slaves. For when its smooth functioning becomes necessary for our survival, its perpetuation, whatever the cost, becomes our most urgent and necessary task. When its smooth functioning depends on a disciplined, rational, careful work force, that which is spontaneous, emotional, exuberant, and unpredictable—those qualities which make up part of our humanity—must be sacrificed. Already, in the debate over nuclear power, such issues are beginning to emerge.

Moreover, the very size of the institutions in the developing global economic system implies regimentation and undermines democracy. In a small organization, people can know each other and through personal contact can participate in decisions of the organization that affect them. To function smoothly, however, a large organization must be hierarchical, bureaucratic, and in some measure impersonal. The more large institutions dominate our lives, the more we will find the conditions of our lives determined by distant others with whom we have no influence.[11] The people of Appalachia and Montana may be as helpless to prevent the strip mining of their region as the inhabitants of New England mill towns have been to prevent distant money managers from closing their mills. In this age of cheap and abundant energy, we feel as powerless to affect the decisions of Exxon as of OPEC. We can feel the edge of the old saw that technological advance does not give power to people generally, but gives some people greater power over many other people.

The Strategy for a High-Energy Future

The age of cheap and abundant fossil fuels draws to a close. The needs of the future require that we begin the construction of a new energy system which depends on another energy source. This task will take a generation or more. Meanwhile, government and business leaders have a strategy which would maintain and extend the American high-energy life style and the institutions on which it now depends. The ingredients of this strategy include developing nuclear power and synthetic fuels, strip mining western coal, importing oil and liquefied natural gas until sometime in the middle of the next century, when fusion power is expected to be commercially feasible and its reactors are constructed. The costs of this program are prodigious. Barry Commoner estimates that investment of capital for the necessary expansion of nuclear power, coal gasification and liquefied natural gas imports in the seven years between 1978 and 1985 will be one trillion dollars. We will pay environmental costs as well in the form of stripped landscapes, polluted waterways, marine oil slicks and smog. We will pay the human costs in increased regimentation and rising cancer deaths.

This strategy carries with it high risks as well. Fusion power though thought ultimately feasible by some scientists as a source of unlimited clean energy has not yet proven itself. Engineering problems may yet come to light which prevent it ever from becoming the

panacea for our energy dilemmas. In generating nuclear power, both
light water fission reactors and breeder reactors could cause cata-
strophic accidents. Increased use of fossil fuels over the next century
could tip the balance of the equilibrium of the global environment
and cause a massive and disastrous change of climate.

Chart 1

Where Are We Going?
A Brief History*

Type of Society	Kilocalories Energy Use Daily	Human Maintenance Levels
Hunting and gathering	2,000	1
Wood-burning	4-5,000	2
Primitive agricultural villages	12,000	6
Advanced agricultural, Middle Ages (water and wind power)	25,000	12
Industrial England (mining, steam engine)	60-70,000	30-35
U.S. technological society (petroleum-based)	230,000	115 times what it takes to maintain human life

*Data from Charles Thomas, in Mark Reader (ed.), *Energy and the Human Dimension*,
Arizona State University Center for Environmental Studies, pp. 66-68.

To be successful this strategy will require not only huge amounts
of investment capital and the willingness to take these risks but also
a degree of coordination and a sense of urgency far beyond what we
have yet shown. Nevertheless, in a somewhat fragmentary fashion
this strategy has won the commitment of most of those in the seats
of power today. And it has won, up to this point, the uneasy
acquiescence of the American people.

One can explain, for all its costs and risks, our commitment to this
high-consumption energy strategy as the result of institutional and
political inertia. Those responsible for energy conglomerates, utilities,
appliance manufactures and nuclear engineering want their organi-

zations to flourish and grow. The implementation of this strategy will enhance that goal. And since the leaders in the energy industry today have both economic and political power, expert knowledge and a record of success, they have a major, if not decisive, voice in determining the energy strategy for the future. And since their wealth and power buy them a major voice in the media, they can tell their story persuasively and broadcast it widely.

Bacon

But perhaps the reasons for our commitment to this strategy are less obvious or simple. A high-energy life style seems to appeal to some deeply felt psychological needs. Such needs find expression in dreams and visions and finally in literature and art. The vision of Francis Bacon pervades industrial culture. In his *New Atlantis*, Bacon pictures people in a Utopian state of the future, endlessly improving the human condition by mastering the material world through the study of nature and applying that new knowledge in improved technology. In this statement he had none of the traditional ambivalence about scientific discovery or the acquisition of power. He had none of the alchemists' concern that he must be spiritually pure and disciplined in order to be a worthy receptacle of new knowledge. Although he predated Descartes, like Descartes he clearly separated himself from his environment, his thought from natural phenomena. By putting nature on a rack we can learn her secrets, he asserted. By learning her secrets we can at last control the conditions of our lives. He had no doubt that, on balance, power gained would be used for good rather than for evil. In so judging he ignored the predominantly military cast of technological development in the past and the Christian teaching about sin. As a father of modern science, Bacon's blind spots have become the blind spots of modern society. In like measure, his aspirations have become ours and have made the scientific and technological enterprise a moral quest. "Better living through chemistry" is a slogan worthy of his pen. And so our society tends to assume that the development of new sophisticated energy technology and an annual increase in our per capita energy consumption will improve the human condition.

Bruegel

A second vision has come out of the closet since the decline of Puritan prejudices and the rise of the consumer society. We can find its symbol in Peter Bruegel's sixteenth-century painting, *The Land of Cockayne*. Here the artist portrays the medieval fantasy of a land

where every whim and appetite find indulgence. In this land, unmit-
igated pleasure can be enjoyed without struggle, self-discipline or
hangover. E. M. Forster's short story, "The Machine Stops," offers
a modern technological version of the same vision.[12] In it he describes
a futurist society so designed that all individuals have their own
private living cubicle loaded with devices which supply food, rest,
information, communication, and pleasure at the touch of a finger.
Advertising often gives the impression that advancing technology
and a high-energy life style can in like manner fulfill our every wish.
In so doing it appeals to the age-old longing to return to Eden.
Psychologists hypothesize that the dream of returning to Eden is the
unconscious longing to return to that blissful state of infancy where
the universe consisted of mother and self; her breast supplied all food
and her hands ministered to all other needs and the warmth of her
body furnished a sense of security and cozy oneness. To grow beyond
infancy, the child must suffer the pain of expulsion from Paradise,
enter a life of struggle, self-definition, and labor, at the end of which
waits death. A high-energy life style offers instant gratification in the
form of fast foods, electronic entertainment, high-speed travel, air
conditioning and central heating, pain-killing drugs and labor-saving
machinery. A promise to lift from the backs of the sons and daughters
of Adam the curse of endless toil is its greatest pride. Even if the
gates of Eden remain securely guarded, a high-energy life style offers
an address in the same neighborhood.

Babel

The third vision completes the trinity. In covenanting together to
build the Tower of Babel, men aspired to make themselves like gods.
Less moral than Bacon's but more heroic than Bruegel's, this vision
invested human beings with the special vocation to overcome biological limits, to extend the boundaries of human knowledge, power and
experience to the utmost bounds of the unfettered imagination,
regardless of the cost. For those addicted to this vision the space
program, the supersonic transport, and the development of fusion
power take on an almost religious dimension. But these infinite
aspirations are still enclosed in finite flesh. Theologians identify the
contradiction as the seedbed of sin and the birthplace of religion.[13]

Furthermore, the certainty of our own death always lurks on the
fringes of consciousness. In his book, *The Denial of Death*,[14] Ernest
Becker argues that since we know we are to die and are therefore
doomed to live in a tragic and terrifying world, the situation calls for

new heroisms which are basically matters of belief and will, dedicated to a vision. "But modern man is drinking and drugging himself out of awareness or he spends his time shopping, which is the same thing." In his chapter in *Ecology, Crisis and New Vision,* John Snow makes a similar point.[15] Using an overweight middle-aged plumber as a model of us all, he describes his high-energy life style and the tremendous use of gadgets and machinery—from power steering to the electronically opening garage doors. In almost imperceptible ways all these energy-consuming tools give him a small but important sense of power and a slight feeling of immortality to shield him momentarily from that gnawing awareness of mortality.

The vision of Babel, to be like gods, includes not only freedom from human finitude and death, but also repudiation of the smelly messy transient fleshiness of our own bodies. Bodies originate in the earth. They feel hunger and thirst. They eat and drink and defecate. They fall sick, they deteriorate with age and die and rot in the dirt. They also generate passions and irrational emotions and "lower" impulses. They engender lust, lechery, and fornication. How could anyone with a body like this succeed in becoming like a god? According to the Western religious tradition God is spiritual, not fleshly. He is rational, not emotional. He has no bodily needs, Jesus to the contrary. But he is masculine nevertheless. Traditional Christian piety has grown from these premises to minimize bodily experience in the lives of the devout, particularly those pleasurable experiences that affirm the body. Bring the body under subjection, runs the advice. Eat as little as possible, just to sustain life. And if the food does not taste good, so much the better. Don't go naked. And don't wear clothes that make one feel attractive and good. Since sensuality is sin and passions are unruly, let reason order your life. Above all, avoid sexual activity or even sexual thoughts. In spite of the church's official approval of sex in marriage, that approval has always been strained and uncomfortable. Alan Watts observed that as far as he knew, never has a stained-glass window of a married couple making love ever graced a Christian church. A very few years ago a flood of angry phone calls protested a clergyman's suggestion on a TV interview that Jesus had a penis.

Christian culture, taking the lead from some of the church fathers, has projected these ungodlike aspects of human nature onto women. Just as the body must be kept under subjection, so should women.[16] It is fitting perhaps that a woman poet, Jane Stembridge, should identify this anti-body bias in American culture:

There are certain jobs
in which the body bends.
Many people
aren't prepared to bend,
They don't like to—
and very often they
can't
So they prefer
the other jobs
and chairs.
They say "these jobs are
            higher class. Man
            should use his mind."
The reason
they like to talk a lot about
THE MIND
is
because they think
the body's VERY
BAD
They never let it loose
to run and play and
prance and dance and
flip and flop
and feel.
They buckle it
and girdle it and
sit it
in a chair.
But
if
the body's buckled up,
the mind is
buckled too.

O
Everything would happen
in
America
if
people should suddenly
discover their toes.[17]

And so the repudiation of the body and physical work adds weight to our penchant for mechanization. If our bodies are bad, machines are good, and in controlling them both we feel like gods.

We live and make public policy in our industrial culture as if we half-believed these dreams to be real. We pursue scientific research as if the knowledge gained would improve rather than threaten human well-being. We try to organize our lives as if a return to Eden were almost possible, and as if certain attributes of divinity were within our grasp. We talk and plan as if industrial civilization will continue forever. Such pretense has a long lineage. The Pharaohs and emperors of antiquity seemed to believe in their own divinity. The Greeks observed that those whose ambitions and success raised them too high suffered a fatally distorted perception of reality called hubris. This led to a form of madness which inevitably resulted in their downfall. The Greek word for it was catastrophe.

The Light-Energy Alternative*
An alternative does exist. The strategy for its implementation has only begun to take shape. It does not demand a sudden end to the importation of petroleum, the mining of coal, or the generation of electric power by nuclear reactors. Instead, it calls for a steady transition to an energy system based on the use of decentralized energy production from several renewable sources, such as solar, wind, hydro and biomass. Since all these technologies together would produce energy neither as plentiful or as cheap as fossil fuels, they could not ever supply our needs without stringent energy conservation measures and the evolution of a satisfying light-energy life style for the whole population. At the end, such a strategy might make possible an arrest in environmental deterioration and the establishment and maintenance of satisfying and egalitarian human communities for long into the future.[18]

The shelf full of new books and the discovery of modern relevance in earlier writings lays the basis for a possible culture of a light-energy society. Certain main features already stand out. Fundamental must be the recognition and acceptance of human creatureliness. This means an abandonment of the aspiration to surpass human limits

---

*The term light energy has been chosen as the opposite of high energy in order to avoid the pejorative connotations of "low" energy, which implies to many people a decline in human activity and the quality of life and a return to a sluggish primitivism. On the contrary, the light-energy alternative might bring an expenditure of somewhat less mechanical energy but must involve greater human activity. It aims at improving the quality of life and requires a broader base and a greater degree of scientific and technical sophistication than the high-energy alternative.

and of the pretense that the gaining of power will not bring with it the temptation, often irresistible, to misuse it. This must not mean an end of the scientific enterprise, but rather a careful directing of science and technical applications to those activities which will really improve the quality of human life. Mortality remains the greatest measure of human limitation, and a light-energy culture must find ways to help people face their terrors and sorrows regarding their own and their loved ones' death. At the same time it must reconcile us to our own deaths without denigrating our bodies. The use of the phrase "our vile bodies" in the Church of England funeral service attempts to buy reassurance at too high a price. The neo-Freudian Norman O. Brown and the feminist Dorothy Dinnerstein each in their own way seek to rehabilitate the body as an entity we can affirm. For all his avoidance of sex, Saint Benedict, in his Rule, affirms the body in a way unusual even today. The holy life for him involved physical labor as well as prayer. Rather than considering labor Adam's curse which technology can and should rescind, he judged it to be a necessary part of the human condition and an ingredient in full and holy living.

"Small is Beautiful" has become a slogan to hint at the second main feature of a light-energy culture. In their various ways not only E. F. Schumacher but Lewis Mumford, Ivan Illich, Wendell Berry, Leopold Kohr and others have explicated themes praising the small, stable, self-reliant face-to-face community. A high-energy civilization requires big institutions to produce and distribute the energy. And big institutions cannot be managed without hierarchical structures, claims Schumacher. In a small community the possibility exists for an egalitarian community. The high-energy future toward which we are currently moving will demand increasing regimentation and a diminution of our control over our own lives. A light-energy future might afford both greater freedom and more influence in the decisions that affect us. Large institutions and large, mobile but concentrated populations increasingly characteristic of our high-energy society become increasingly impersonal and bureaucratic. The values of a life shared with our spouse instead of a succession of lovers might be paralleled by the values of a few lifelong friends instead of a large number of temporary acquaintances. Most important, a light-energy society would not require a progressive devastation of the environment to support it. It would therefore be sustainable. Some cultures of American Indians chose as their goal to live so as to produce the least possible impact on their environment. Such an ambition might become part of a light-energy culture. This could lead to an intimate knowledge of one's own neighborhood, which might through the years bring more satisfaction and pleasure than a flight across the Atlantic or a coast-to-coast tour. Edgar Anderson, a botanist, remembers as one of his happiest summers the one which he spent with a grass identification book and hand lens in the middle of a large field. Howard Evans, an entomologist, recently discovered in his own backyard three species of insects never before known to science.

One thing a light-energy society would not have is the excitement of the gigantic feats of engineering and the speed and variety and drama with which our high-energy civilization has fed us. The moon landing, the skyscrapers, the world series, the great crowds watching fireworks and hearing the orchestra on the riverbank, add spice and entertainment to lives that might otherwise seem to hold little meaning. Without circuses as well as bread, life can be dull, unless a people can learn to find meaning in the small familiar things of the concrete here and now. Tennyson saw as much when he addressed his ode to the flower in a crannied wall and imagined that to understand that flower would be to understand the whole of creation. Luther said more when he related that one Christmas Eve, while kneeling in church, he felt the overwhelming sense that the Christ knelt behind him. Giving in to his impulse to peek brought him face to face with an ordinary peasant saying his prayers. In this he realized the glory of the Incarnation. It must have been a poetic Celt who described the holy isle of Iona off the west coast of Scotland as "a thin place." By that he meant that there the membrane between the temporal and the eternal, the material and the spiritual world, was unusually thin. The consensus of the great mystics is that in spite of appearances there is no membrane. In the face of multiplicity there is unity. In the midst of differences and conflicts there is connectedness and harmony.

Jesus addressed a culture which stood on the edge of the greatest empire of the ancient world. The values of the empire, with its glorying in bigness, power, wealth, glamor, luxury, and sophistication, seeped into the Jewish culture of Galilee. One could argue that Jesus preached a light-energy ethic consistent with the culture of the wandering desert tribes, the culture of the judges, the prophets, and the common people. He was posing against the ethic of the Roman Empire the ethic of the Kingdom of God.[19]

Considerations like these, though beginning with a decision about energy policy, soon become a question about the meaning of human life. Whether the potentials and constraints of a light-energy culture can meet the deep psychic needs addressed by our high-energy contemporary society remains to be seen. Whether a high-energy society can for long preserve humane conditions is much in doubt. The choice of paths is in part ours.

Chapter 3:

Energy as a Moral and Religious Issue

*by Alvin Pitcher**

In the United States we use the wrong kind of energy, we use energy in the wrong way, and we make our decisions about energy, economically and politically, the wrong way. In other words, we act immorally or unethically in relation to energy. Our use of energy is a moral or an ethical issue.[1] We have also developed an energy technology and an energy producing, processing, and distributing system that undermines democratic politics. This makes energy a political issue, as the next chapter will show. We also want too much energy. Our way of being, our life style, requires too much energy to sustain it. That points to a crisis of religious meaning.

Even if we were to use more renewable sources of energy, use our energy more efficiently, make our decisions about energy in the light of a national program that embodies a notion of the common good, and change the energy producing, processing, and distributing system accordingly, we would still confront an underlying issue, namely that we use so much energy, in part, because our way of life is idolatrous. It is not fulfilling. The high use of energy is in part a response to our failure to find adequate meaning in life.

*Formerly Associate Professor of Ethics and Society, Divinity School, University of Chicago; currently Minister of Christian Community Development, University Church, Chicago.

One could almost say that our way of life is organized in such a way as to use energy. The energy producers and related forces in our country foster a way of life that uses their products. This is both a self-conscious sponsorship and the unconscious result of working through the images and symbols that constitute our sense of well-being and fulfillment.

I. We Use the Wrong Kind of Energy

If we believed that the resources of the earth were a part of the creation, gifts of God for all life, human and otherwise, we would use resources so that all life, present and future, had access to needed resources and so that threats to life from the polluting effects of the use of resources were minimized. Thus we would use nonrenewable energy resources sparingly and concentrate on the use of resources that are renewable. Only with extreme caution would we use energy sources that produce gases, particles, radiation, and heat, excesses of which threaten the survival of life. We would use gas, oil, coal, and fission and fusion sources which leave radioactive residues or contaminated materials less and less or not at all. We would use sun, wind, and water more and more. One of the ways to use the sun, now almost completely neglected, would be to grow organic material and convert it to alcohol or gas.[2]

Even in our use of fossil fuels we somehow decide to use what is in shortest reserve. Thus, every year, we consume 3.6 billion barrels of domestically produced oil out of reserves of roughly 200 billion barrels (to use a fairly optimistic estimate), 22 trillion cubic feet of natural gas out of reserves of about 500 trillion cubic feet, and 600 million tons of coal out of reserves of about 1500 billion tons. With all the problems of producing and using coal, many of which could be at least partially eliminated by the introduction of better technologies (Sweden's fluidized bed for burning coal all but eliminates pollution), it makes more sense to use coal rather than oil and gas. The ratios of use to reserve are 1 to 56 for oil, 1 to 23 for gas, and 1 to 2500 for coal.

My perception of what is going on may be one-sided, but I experience two quite different approaches to the use of energy. One group of people believes, and exerts tremendous pressure on the government and on our minds by advertising and so-called education, in a program which emphasizes the discovery of new sources of oil, gas, coal, and fissionable materials and new technologies for using them. What is needed is more of the nonrenewable sources, they say;

what is needed is more supply of the same. They are not able, perhaps because of the mental climate created by years of thinking in a certain way, to understand and support the movement toward renewable resources. Most federal and state policies have favored the development of this approach to all energy issues.

Another group of people, mostly individual citizens or small groups of people without much money or power, favors a dramatic change in our policies, with research and development money shifting drastically toward renewable resources, with all kinds of government incentives to entice people and institutions to use renewable sources of energy. This group may be a little blind to the short-term needs of the economic system for continued use of nonrenewable sources, but their general push toward long-term dependency on renewable resources and their support of present policies that aid and abet such development seem to me to be morally preferable. California seems to be one state with a government that perceives the situation in this way and has had some power to move in this direction.

While moral decisions are usually somewhat ambiguous, I am convinced that there is no real choice for the morally sensitive person but to be on the side of those pushing vigorously for the shift toward renewable and nonpolluting resources now! There are many decisions involved in moving in this direction. We will be discussing some of these in the section on economics and politics.

II. We Use Energy the Wrong Way

If we believed that the resources of the earth were a part of the creation, gifts of God for all life, human and otherwise, we would use resources carefully, with a minimum of waste, and hence with a maximum of effectiveness. The very least we would do is to use energy efficiently. We would use energy so as to get more work out of the energy we use. We would build our houses into the sides of hills, face them south, insulate them well, use heat pumps, build cars that use less gasoline, build public transportation systems, arrange work, shopping, and residential areas so that less energy is needed for transportation, recycle almost everything, generate much of our electricity where the heat can be used for heating buildings and in industrial processes, and encourage efficient industrial technology. We would encourage pricing policies which, contrary to most present practice, charge more for electricity during the peak load periods daily and seasonally. We would use money incentives, government regulation, and educational programs to encourage patterns of energy use which obtain more work from the same amount of energy. We would exercise our moral responsibility to become much more energy-efficient.

We can stop using energy in a way that heavily pollutes the air and the water. Swedish technologists have developed a way of burning coal, the fluidized bed process, which virtually eliminates pollution, with the exception of the carbon dioxide given off in burning. Scrubbers and other devices can be employed and are more and more used, albeit reluctantly. Cogeneration of electricity and of heat to be used in heating and cooling buildings and water, and in industrial processes, would reduce the thermal polluting effects on our lakes and streams and air.

Although the net effect of thermal pollution and of particles or gas in the atmosphere on the heating or cooling of the earth is "up for grabs" among scientists, the resulting interference with natural rhythms and cycles is sufficiently important to cause us to stop letting things develop as they will. If we recognized inorganic and organic limits or boundaries established in the created order of things, we would not let energy technologies develop without trying to take the limits into account.

In addition to using energy in an inefficient and polluting manner, we have used energy in such a way that its technology requires large amounts of capital, concentrated economic and hence political power, and small amounts of manpower.

Here again we find two quite different approaches to the energy issue. Those who push for increase in the supply of traditional fossil fuels or for nuclear energy tend to ignore the importance of the efficient, less polluting use of energy. While they may give lip service to the ideas, it is apparent that they are not very interested in them. We can understand why persons and institutions devoted to increasing sales and profits would not have a material interest in decreasing the demand for their products, but it is lamentable that such a perspective is the one that is most often presented in the public media, and the one that possesses the money and the staff to represent its interests so powerfully in the legislative processes. To an increasing number of people, it does not make sense to pay tens of billions to import oil and to suffer the economic and political pangs of such payments and dependency if we could get 40 percent more work from our oil, thereby decreasing our use from 6570 million barrels a year to 4693 million barrels, and our yearly imports from about 2900 million barrels to about 1100 million barrels. Saving about billions of dollars on imports, the positive effects of this on our balance of payments and on the strength of the dollar in foreign exchange, are so obvious and important that it is hard to see how anyone could be against such a program if the interests of the whole society were dominant in making decisions. Clearly, it is irresponsible to continue to use oil as inefficiently as we are. It is also irresponsible to use as much pollution-increasing energy as we do.

The group advocating the efficient, less polluting use of energy is gaining strength.

In order to use energy more efficiently and with less pollution, those who assume moral responsibility will become a part of two movements, one more personal and private, one more social and public. Individuals can begin to support the efficient and less polluting use of energy by buying cars that get more miles per gallon of gasoline, by car pooling, by using more public transportation, by fostering programs in homes, churches, and other institutions for energy savings, by recycling materials, by becoming aware of the efficiency ratios of all energy-using appliances, such as refrigerators, air conditioners, washers, and dryers, and by becoming aware of the great inefficiency of using electricity for heating and cooling water or air. The all-electric home is clearly a very poor supporter of the efficient use of energy. Building such a home seems to me to be irresponsible.

As citizens, we are also responsible for public policies that would encourage or require an increase in the efficiency with which we use energy. Policies which increase the price of energy and thereby tend to encourage its efficient use are morally desirable, if the adverse effects of such policies on persons with low incomes and on the attempt to control inflation do not offset the advantages.

We should not have to avoid what is desirable for energy because we have not dealt with the issue of low income generally. In other words we should face the problem of low economic income primarily by other means. When we do not, there is considerable pressure to avoid any energy policy which works a hardship on those with low incomes. Meanwhile, we can at least provide the "life-line" energy policies which guarantee a modest amount of energy at modest prices for everyone. Heating, lighting, and transportation energy supplies could be guaranteed at reasonable prices for private use. Large users would thus bear the weight of the effect of increased costs. Of course, everyone who purchases anything other than life-line energy would bear the increased costs that are currently passed along to consumers. An alternative to using price and the market mechanism for securing increased efficiency is to impose standards of efficiency by legislative or administrative action. Congress has already set standards for automobile manufacturers which will require an average of 27.5 miles per gallon by 1985. All kinds of economic incentives could be offered to those who institute efficient uses of energy.

Any abstract consideration of a desirable mechanism for securing efficiency must be balanced by the political possibility of securing its adoption. Imposition of standards seems the fairest for consumers, but this involves all the problems of bureaucratic control. Economic incentives combine imposition with a large amount of freedom to respond. While some would argue that the market if left to itself would solve the problems most equitably, I am convinced that it has not and will not react in time or adequately take into account the issues we face.

The use of energy is a moral issue, and it is irresponsible not to move personally and publicly toward policies and programs that use energy more efficiently. We have an ethical responsibility to decide among the various paths for public policy, to advocate such policies, and to work for such compromises as seem necessary in order to get more efficient, less polluting uses of energy. We must, however, be careful not to advocate one path so strenuously that no new path is taken.

III. We Make Our Economic and Political Decisions About Energy in the Wrong Way

If we believed that the resources of the earth were a part of the creation, gifts of God for all life, human and otherwise, we would use resources so that all life, present and future, has access to needed resources, and so that threats to life from the polluting effects of the use of energy are minimized. And we would make our economic and political decisions about energy from such a perspective. We would also organize our relations to energy in such a way that the economic and political processes provided meaningful participation. What is most obvious and indisputable is that we do not make our economic and political decisions with any such perspective as the dominant one. Some will argue, and not without grounds, that the best way to take into account the interests of all of the people in the United States is to let the market system function economically and the democratic political system function politically. Critics of our system insist that large corporations, the military, large trade unions, large trade associations, and an entrenched government bureaucracy generally exert such pressure that the will of the people is never developed or exerted enough to be effective. While the system functions better than the critics often admit in the short term in some areas, the market economy has *not* taken into account the social costs of using energy the way we have, the long-term needs for renewable sources of energy, the condition of millions of people around the world whose resources do not permit them to enter the market in a significant way, and the political consequences of concentrations of economic power acting a good deal of the time without constraints other than profit. Can such economic enterprise be counted upon to adhere voluntarily to larger goals and interests? Even when governments have imposed constraints, large concentrations of power have frequently been able to circumvent the restraints and to act virtually as autonomous entities or, in cooperation with other economic groups, to act very much like transnational powers without a need to consider national interests.

Alternatives, however, are not simple. In my judgment, the system would not function adequately simply by becoming freer from the collusions of large concentrations. It is not enough to appeal to a democratic system in which we depend for justice and humanity upon the freely expressed interests of autonomous individuals. How does a perspective which provides, for both the economic and political systems, an informing concern for and vision of the good of all persons or of all of life, come about? While at times the citizenry as a whole has come down on the side of what seems clearly a long-term good, at times it seems to vote economically and politically for 70-mile-per-hour speed limits, or no speed limit, big cars, low prices for energy, and for other measures which are ethically short-sighted, rather than for environmental protection. Unless the character of the people is such that they desire more focus on renewable, efficient, nonpolluting energy, and a way of life which requires less of it, there is no guarantee that a morally desirable energy program and practice will be the result of more citizen participation in economic and political decisions.*

I conclude that neither our theory nor our practice in the economic and political dimensions of life is morally defensible. To be responsible in economic and political matters is to find a way to implement the principles, programs, and practices that issue from the perspective

---

*If we took seriously the imperative of the American democratic tradition that an informed electorate is responsible, with the help of the Constitution and the Supreme Court which protects the Constitution and hence the people themselves, we would certainly increase the emphasis on an informed public or on informed publics. In considering energy policy, Swedish leaders sponsored ten thousand group discussions of at least ten hours in which 80,000 people participated.

emerging in our discussion, one in which the long-term life of the planet is taken into account and in which the needs of all life are met with some measure of equity and humaneness. There is no guarantee that either the people or the government will embody such a perspective as things stand now. Therefore any program or policy which does not take into account the character or the being of the people, or of the leaders who function for the people, is inadequate. It is not only a question of an interest in justice or of equity for all life. It is also a question of the content of equity or justice. It is also, therefore, a religious question. The Christian religious perspective leads me to the judgment that we use too much energy in our way of living. And our way of producing and distributing energy threatens some of our cherished political institutions. But before I discuss energy as a religious issue there is a different sense in which energy involves politics.

Energy Technology as a Political Issue

We have an energy producing, processing, and distributing system that requires large investments of capital, technological sophistication, and concentrations of economic power and hence of political power—all of which make it very difficult for ordinary or even extraordinary folk to know enough to make judgments about policy and to have the means to influence policy, at least in comparison to the industry.

To the extent that we use solar energy with a simple technology, we will be better able to understand and to control our source of energy. But if we develop satellites to collect the sun's rays, which are then beamed back to earth, we have not changed the political meaning of the energy system. Likewise, if we develop large collecting systems which feed into the general energy grid, we will not have affected the politics of energy or the informal structure of our political system—that is, the way the system operates regardless of what the formal institutions provide to enhance citizen participation.

If we encourage wind power, and small biomass-converting technologies for producing alcohol or methane gas, some people could become energy self-sufficient. If our cities were deconverted so as to have living units of about 200,000 people, we could further develop energy production systems with less concentration of capital and power. There is no guarantee that the new technologies would foster better politics. But technologies such as the generation of heat and power combined with the local use of sun, wind, and water could work for the decentralization of the energy industry.

IV. We Use Too Much Energy

If we believed that the resources of life as well as our own lives were provided in continuous creation as gifts of God, we would not only act as good stewards of the resources for the sake of all life present and future, but we would also attend to the created limits or givens of life and listen to what that reality says regarding the way we now live. In other words, we would accept the limits not simply as something to be overcome or adjusted to reluctantly, but also as symbols of the meaning of our being and as guideposts for human fulfillment. Our overuse of energy reveals that the way of being or the life style that dominates our society is questionable.

We have organized our lives in a way that requires a whole complex of attitudes, behaviors, and institutions which misuse energy. For example, we have organized our lives so that the human body is not required to be called upon by the ordinary activities of the day, except in very limited ways. As a result we now have all kinds of health clubs, health programs, jogging jags, yoga sessions and much else—all of which is therapeutic. That is to say, it comes as a response to the destructive or debilitating effects of the normal patterns of most people's lives. Hence we develop a whole range of activities, some expensive and time-consuming and usually somewhat artificial—they are not really play—in order to offset the effects of the system of life. If the system of life were different, there would be little need for such activities. For example, if towns had populations of about 200,000 and were organized with industry, housing, shopping and other facilities that supported the population within their borders, one could walk or bike to work, to shop, to church, to school, and thus use the body more in the normal course of living. If there were more time, opportunity, and freedom to play, "artificial" body activity would not need to be found. The use of energy, especially of nonhuman energy, is associated with a way of life which requires long transportation to almost everything.

The situation is the same with regard to the energy embodied in goods and services.* While it is clear that, per dollar expended, electricity (502,500 BTUs per dollar) and gasoline and oil (430,700 BTUs per dollar) are by far the most energy-intensive, goods and services also embody energy inputs. For example, kitchen and house-hold appliances involve 58,700 BTUs per dollar spent; new and used cars, 55,600; furniture, 36,700; women's and children's clothing, 33,100; men's and boys' clothing, 31,400; restaurants, 32,400; private

---

*See Appendix B

hospitals, 26,100; tobacco products, 19,800; telephone and telegraph, 19,000. Thus a society that does not provide satisfactions in work and other more or less routine activities of living encourages the increased use of goods and services in order to secure psychic satisfactions otherwise denied.

Much of what goes on in modern society is an effort to compensate for the destructive or nonfulfilling aspects of our present way of life. Many of our health services, physical and mental, are simply trying to make up for the inability of the system to function in a fulfilling way. We spend billions of dollars therapeutically in patch work when those billions could be spent on more basic work, if we had the conception and the will to reorder family, educational, and work reality. We divide up, differentiate or fragment life as much as possible; and we avoid relating one aspect to another except in an external, instrumental way. While the specialized parts are sometimes coordinated or externally related, generally speaking, the whole has become less and less central. One performs a special function on an assembly line, or in a computer center. One finds health care provided by an increasing number of specialists. Knowledge is more and more fragmented, and universities have many departments within which there is further specialization. One is expected to know more and more about particular aspects of smaller dimensions of reality. The functional parts are not expected to explain themselves to each other or to be able to relate themselves to each other except externally— that is, administratively. And one wonders whether or not administrators understand the relation of the parts to some significant whole. The parts are autonomous, laws unto themselves. Political, economic, educational, scientific, technological, and religious dimensions of life are allowed to function autonomously, independently of each other.

As it is with function so it is with meaning, if we can separate such matters. Education is expected to be neutral, to be technical or, at best, to be historically humanistic. Educators are not expected to ask questions of meaning within specialties they are studying. Economic institutions are not expected to ask about the value of their enterprises. Technology has been developed without asking the difficult questions about the effects of its use upon people and environment. Persons are trained and socialized in preparation for the performance of functions within particular segments of the system, without persistent demands to explain the meaning of such functions for the society as a whole, or without question as to their relation to the meaning of life in the society in some ultimate sense. The religious question, the question of ultimate meaning, is ignored or relegated to private or interpersonal matters.

Fragmentation and autonomy are associated with constant change and a sense of freedom from limits. Participation in communities which gives content to one's individual life while at the same time limiting one's freedom is deemphasized. One cannot have too many attachments to communities if one is expected to change one's abode physically and spiritually from time to time in response to the call of one's specialized function. The forms which limit and order life give way to change. The destinies which provide limits—natural, psychological, and spiritual—are subordinated to the freedoms to make and shape almost everything.

Thus, what some hail as the continuing basis of everything modern and good of the past several hundred years—the fragmentation or differentiation and autonomy of function and meaning—must be challenged.

Where now we have fragmentation or individualization, we will foster participation. Where we have focused on parts, we will focus on wholes. Whereas we have lauded change, or whatever is new, we will focus on persisting forms. Whereas we have worshipped freedom, we will recognize the crucial role of the givens that set limits to our freedoms. Whereas we have concentrated on meaning in a kind of horizontal, historical reality, we will move toward meaning that transcends history, that does not focus on what we can do and make.

Nevertheless, while we move toward these new emphases, the creative contributions of modern life are not to be denied or ignored. Life and health require both individualization and participation, both part and whole, both change and persisting form, both freedom and attention to the givens, both concerns for meaning in history and for meaning that transcends history, both surface and depth dimensions.

In this interpretation, history is viewed as a movement which involves shifts of emphasis. In our particular period, the undue focus on the individual, on change, on freedom, and on the historical must be offset by a rigorous radical movement toward participation, forms, givens, and realities below the surface of life.

The situation as I have described it characterizes life in the United States, in Canada, in many European countries, in Japan, in Australia, and to a great extent in the Soviet Union. Socialism represents an effort to overcome some of the destructiveness present in the life style of modernity. It represents a response to the problems created by an excessive emphasis on freedom and individualization, but the movement as a whole has not recognized the character of the issues created by the technological revolution and the loss of depth. Looking at many places in the world, one must admit the need for some of the creative results of modernization. The issues become somewhat different in Third World countries. There the issue is to free the nation for development without buying into what now appear to be the destructive consequences of modern society. The issue in the developed nations is how to create a new framework in the face of a seemingly all-encompassing reality which contains the seeds of its own destruction.

Sometimes one thinks that the only hope lies in helping others to avoid a total commitment to the principles of modernity. The forces unleashed by modernity, once allowed full sway, seem unbreachable. How, for example, is one to find a way to preserve a meaningful extended family—a blood community—in the light of the fact that increasing differentiation of functions and specialized training for these functions leads individual members of families to move about the globe?

V. Responses to the Moral, Political, and Religious Issues

A Moral Response

Each of us can begin to use different kinds of energy, to use energy more efficiently, and to participate in economic and political processes that move toward the encouragement of the energy practices and policies recommended above. There are many inventories and illustrations of the kinds of actions individuals and small groups have found helpful.[3]

Some people are in a position to use solar energy, either in retrofitting existing buildings, in the rehabilitation of buildings, or in new construction. Some persons can do this for their own living space. Others are in a position within churches, businesses, schools, clubs, unions, or other institutions, to influence decisions. In some cases wind power might be utilized. One technician claims that wind power could produce as much as 300 quadrillion BTUs, or four times as much energy as we are now using from all sources. Money is available through the Department of Energy for experimentation. I know some architects who are building their own solar houses without professional help. They are getting help from the government. A covenantal community from our church is in the process of planning the rehabilitation of an apartment building with twenty apartments, using as much solar power as is economically feasible, and perhaps some that is not yet economically viable. Some people are reestablishing fireplaces and other wood-burning heating units as a means of reducing their dependency on oil, gas, and electricity. Some people are generating electrical power with wind power and are actually feeding it back into the electrical system of the power companies. All of these possibilities are situationally limited.

Having been excluded from the political decisions that led to the development of nuclear energy, many citizens are now politically active in trying to regain some control over the process of energy production, using benign technologies.[4]

An Energy Program for Governmental Agencies: A Political Response

When President Carter called for citizen dialogue about an energy program, I took him seriously. My proposals have to do with five major objectives:[5]

1. The Efficient Use of Energy

Generally speaking, the cost of energy should be allowed to increase by removing price controls at the same time that the federal government establishes an energy tax on all sources at the initial source of supply. This fund would be similar to the Highway Trust Fund, a fund for the development of energy resources and the promotion of efficiency. One proposal is a tax of fifty cents per million BTUs. At the present rate of energy usage, this would net the fund about 38 billion dollars each year. One thing should be clear, however. To remove price controls without providing for public participation in the resulting profits, or to allow or cause the cost of energy to rise without taking into account the economic consequences, would be inhuman.

a. Conservation: Transportation Sector

The aim of the program in the transportation sector would be to increase the mileage per gallon of gasoline for cars and trucks, and to increase the availability of public transportation.

To that end a tax on gasoline should be instituted by the federal government, in addition to the general energy tax. I would try twenty-five cents per gallon immediately, and plan to increase the tax to perhaps seventy-five cents per gallon over the next six years. I would also tax the purchase of new heavier cars with specified mileage ratings (below 20 mph) about a thousand dollars. I would provide a tax credit for the purchase of cars with very high mileage ratings, e.g., 40 miles per gallon in combined E.P.A. ratings. Such a program creates problems for the lower income people who drive old gas guzzlers, for the handicapped, perhaps, who claim that they need larger cars for their wheelchairs, and for farmers. Yet we cannot put off doing what we need to do to reduce our use of oil for gasoline because of these problems. We have a moral responsibility to deal with them in other ways.

I would tax air transportation—especially under 500 miles—in order to encourage bus and rail travel and heavily subsidize mass transport facilities. Both are necessary in order to get a shift in travel habits. Diesel fuel probably ought to be taxed at a lower rate than gasoline, low enough to encourage its use in trucks and high enough to encourage rail use. All of this entails a lot of interference with things as they are. I favor incentives over regulation and subsidy over tax as much as is feasible.

Let me now indicate or speculate about some of the possible savings from such a program. Savings always have to be viewed both as savings over the present usage and as savings in the light of projected increases in energy usage. Thus, if we have over 90 million cars now, which number we assume will increase by at least 15 million by the year 2000, we might calculate the gasoline usage at 10,000 miles a year per vehicle, at an average of 30 miles per gallon. According to the Energy Policy and Conservation Act, the average mileage of all cars produced is required to be 27.5 miles by 1985. It is therefore reasonable to expect standards of at least 30 miles per gallon by the year 2000. One hundred and five million cars would use 35 billion gallons or .83 billion barrels. This corresponds to 90 million cars using about 1.65 billion barrels at present. We need a program that significantly increases our mileage per gallon of gasoline, that encourages us to use our cars less, and that begins the transition to alcohol as fuel. It seems to me to be a reasonable assumption that by 2000 A.D. we could cut our gasoline consumption by half, or by 4 million barrels per day, or by 1.46 billion barrels per year. In 1976 we used 6.417 billion barrels of oil of which we imported 2.646 billion barrels. The political and economic significance of such a projected saving is obvious. If we pay fifteen dollars per barrel of oil, we are saving $21.9 billion in payments abroad. We are cutting that amount from our own expenditures, and thus raising our standard of living. (I am assuming that efficient cars will cost no more than our present inefficient ones.)

Chart 2

1 quad	=	10^{15} BTU

The metric energy unit is the *joule*

1054.8 joules	=	1 BTU
4.186 J	=	1 gram calorie
4186 J	=	1 kg (kilocalorie)
2,685,600 J	=	1 hp hour
3,600,000 J	=	1 kilowatt hour

U.S. energy consumption (mid-1970s) 75 quads/year

1 quad	=	172 million barrels of oil
1 quad	=	1000 billion cubic feet of bottled gas
1 quad	=	41 million tons of coal

b. Conservation: The Residential Sector

In the residential sector we could discourage the use of electricity and encourage insulation, the use of heat pumps, the use of solar energy for heating and cooling, architectural design that maximizes warming effects in winter and cooling effects in summer, as well as experimentation with community cogeneration of heat and electricity.

Tax credits and low-interest loans would be provided for insulation. Efficiency standards could be part of the specifications of all federal, state, and locally-funded projects (insulation, architectural design, heat pumps). Electrical rates would increase rapidly after reasonable amounts, fast enough to discourage all-electric homes.[6] (We lose two-thirds of the heat value of every cubic foot of gas or gallon of oil or ton of coal converted to electricity.)

In the residential area, we used 16.3 quads in 1973. Usage here, of course, must take into account an increase in population, estimated by the Ford Foundation Energy study at 60 million between 1970 and 2000.[7] I used an increase of 45 million in considering transportation, partly because I think there will be fewer cars per person in 2000 than in 1970. There also will be considerably more doubling up of families and more efficient use of housing units by 2000, so I will use the lower figure (45 million increase) here. Housing units are likely to increase from 63 million in 1970 to 80 million in 1985 to 99 million in 2000. On my lower figure there would be corresponding numbers of 72 million for 1985 and 88 million for 2000. We will be able to use solar energy for space heating, cooling, and heating water

in 25 million new housing units; let us assume that this will be done
in 15 of the 25 million additional new units. Let us also assume that
many old homes can be retrofitted with solar energy, so that we have
a total of 20 million homes using solar energy in addition to insulation
and heat pumps. Let us further assume that we save 80 percent of
traditional energy costs in this way. If we had 63 million units using
about 16.3 quads in 1970, the rate was about .25873 quads per million
housing units, or 258.73 million BTUs per unit. If we can save 80
percent on 20 million units, we will save 4.14 quadrillion BTUs. The
savings result from the use of solar, insulation, and the installation
of heat pumps.

There is no way to calculate the effects of higher prices and
incentives on efficiency. I am assuming that by 2000, 20 million units
of housing might operate with 80 percent of present fuel sources,
thus using 1.035 quads. For the other 68 million units, I assume 65
percent of fuel used in 1970 (65 percent of 206.984 million BTUs
per unit), or 9.15 quads. This is probably optimistic. Hence I use 11
quads as projected demand for 68 million units, and 12 quads for the
88 million units. This does not include the energy from solar. I have
not allowed for the increased rate of usage per household, which
seems to be included in the Ford report figures. Thus, for them, in
1970 we have 158.73 million BTUs per housing unit, and in 2000 we
have 304.04 million, 199.949 million, and 171.717 million BTUs per
unit respectively in their three different scenarios. With the thrust for
conservation and some change in attitude toward the use of resources,
both because of price and of our energy situation, my figures may
not turn out to be as optimistic as they seem even to me.

   c. *Energy Conservation: The Industrial and Commercial Sectors*
In the industrial and commercial sectors, the aim is to promote
cogeneration of electricity, using the heat for heat or for steam in
industrial processes, to increase the use of heat pumps, to encourage
the installation of devices to recuperate heat from industrial processes,
to ensure that all new plants or processes use the most efficient
technologies available, to use recycled materials wherever possible, to
minimize the use of electricity except where cogeneration makes the
use of electricity comparatively efficient, and to increase the efficiency
of space heating and cooling equipment.

In order to achieve these goals we will employ tax credits, low-
interest loans, increased rates for large users of electricity, the general
tax on energy, readjustment of transportation rates on scrap metals
(rates that now favor ore over scrap), electrical rates that promote
off-peak load use of electricity, special tax benefits and loans for the

introduction of new technologies to use coal, and special taxes on oil and gas when used in large quantities.

If we consider the possibilities in the commercial sector, I expect more savings there than in the residential sector, business men and women generally having more capacity and incentive to respond to price changes. But the increase in commercial development is larger per year. In the commercial sector in 1973, electricity made up 4.2 quads in comparison to 6.2 quads for other energy sources. In the projections by the Ford report, the commercial sector will use from 21.3 to 16.9 quads of energy in 2000.

Space heating, air conditioning, and water heating make up respectively 49.8 percent, 55.44 percent, and 57 percent of the energy used in the commercial sector. I see no reason why a good portion of this energy cannot be taken care of by solar installations. Let us assume that with proper incentives, 50 percent of commercial businesses increased their efficiencies by 50 percent, for a total of a 25 percent decrease in energy use. I know that this is arbitrary, but I will decrease the 16.9 quads called for by the Ford study technical growth scenario by 25 percent and schedule the commercial sector for 13.7 quads.

Thus far I have projected energy demands in 2000 at 13.3 quads for transportation, 12 quads for residential and 14 quads for commercial, a total of 39.3 quads.

The sector using the largest amount of energy is the industrial. According to the Ford report, the industrial sector used 29.5 quads in 1973 and will use, according to their three different scenarios, 96.9 quads, 63.1 quads, or 47 quads. In these scenarios electricity makes up respectively 45.6 quads, 14.4 quads, and 15.6 quads. In 1973, industry used 8.1 quads of electricity. Other than electricity, energy use, according to the high historical growth pattern projections, includes 30.8 quads for process steam; direct heat, 10.5 quads; feedstocks, 13.3 quads; and on-site power, 1.2 quads.

There can be no doubt that substantial increases in efficiency are possible in steam generation with the use of the heat pump and with cogeneration, heat recuperation, more efficient industrial processes, and materials recycling. Some of the changes can occur relatively soon; some I have been led to understand will require considerable time.

Very arbitrarily, I am using 60 quads as the figure for the industrial sector in 2000.[8] This gives me a total demand of 99.3 quadrillion BTUs for 2000.

I turn now to consider sources for this energy.

Chart 3

Demand 2000	
Transportation	13.3
Residential	12
Commercial	14
Industrial	60
Total	99.3

2. A Program for the Development of Different Sources of Energy

We should focus our research and development on renewable sources, with a heavy emphasis upon what I will call solar or direct conversion of sunlight into heat or electricity, and bioconversion, the conversion of sunlight into plants and plants into fuel. Equal emphasis should be placed on these two sources, although my own present inclination is to favor bioconversion. Additional research would be focused on thermal gradients—waves, geothermal, and wind.[9] I place them in this second order of priority because thermal gradients seem less likely to be viable technologically and economically than do bioconversion and direct solar. A third level of research and development would focus on research for fission, fusion, use of oil shale, gasification and liquefaction of coal. Since these latter sources are at present not part of my long-term program, I assume that, with adequate conservation and development of bioconversion and solar directly, we will not need them in the intermediate stages of a shift away from coal, gas and oil.

We are using energy today roughly at the rate of 75 quadrillion BTUs per year. That is the equivalent of 3 billion tons of coal. We are using somewhere between 600 and 700 million tons of coal per year. Seventy-five quadrillion BTUs, or 75 quads, as some people refer to the figure, is the equivalent of about 13 billion barrels of oil. In 1976, we used oil at the rate of about 7.3 billion barrels of oil per year. Seventy-five quads of energy is the equivalent of about 80 trillion cubic feet of natural gas. We have been consuming about 25 trillion cubic feet per year.

What are we going to substitute for the oil, and coal, and gas that now make up almost all of our energy resources? What can we expect from bioconversion? Very tentatively I estimate that by 2000, if not before, we could secure the following amounts of energy from bioconversion processes:

Chart 4

1. Urban wastes[10]	1 quadrillion BTUs
2. Forest and mill residues[11]	4 quads
3. Agricultural residues[12]	4 quads
4. Use of algae in feeding and use of released forage lands—40 million acres[13]	6 quads
5. Growth of trees on 175 million acres unused at present—20 inches of rainfall annually[14]	10 quads
6. Ocean farming—one kelp farm of 470 square miles[15]	7.5 quads
7. Acres released by eating grains and not feeding grains to cattle and pigs (100 million)	10 quads
8. Other programs, such as treatment of sewerage with water hyacinths and use of water hyacinths growing in river beds, etc.[16]	———
Total	42.5 quads

A conservative estimate of the possible energy from biomass sources is included in my projections for the year 2000 at 26.5 quadrillion Btus. This is 16 quads less than a scaled-down total of the totals that researchers estimate. Hence, I use 49.3 quads less than one could project if one takes the most optimistic researcher's estimates (75.8 quads). I do not include some sources which are claimed to be available by researchers.

Using the 26.5 quads from biomass, and including somewhat conservative estimates from other sources, we might expect to secure 99.6 quads of energy from the following sources in the year 2000.[17] (See chart 5).

3. Shift Use of Oil and Gas to Coal and Clean Up Use of Coal

We can get this shift by providing tax incentives and low-interest loans for such changes. Sweden seems to have developed a process for burning coal which is much cleaner than traditional methods, a technology that can be used in small and large furnaces. A tax on large users of oil and gas would encourage the shift. Mining under

Chart 5

Energy Needs From Combined Sources, Year 2000*

Biomass		26.5 quadrillion BTUs
Wind		6
Hydroelectric		3
Geothermal		5
Solar		10
Coal	900 million tons	22.5
Oil	2 billion barrels (1976 total of 6.417 billion brls, 3.767 billion brls domestic)	11.6
Gas	15 trillion cubic feet	15
	Total	99.6

*Compare appendix C.

very strict environmental and safety standards, while costly, is possible, according to some students of the issues.

4. Assure Every Citizen of Reasonable Energy Supplies for Cooking, Heating, and Lighting at Reasonable Prices

We should treat the provision of fuel for heating the way we treat electricity, by making such provision a function of a public utility. Under present statutes, I think the states can provide life-line programs in electricity wherein every citizen is entitled to receive a certain amount of electricity at minimum rates. Rates increase with further use. I am sure that there is a way to provide heating fuel on a similar basis. Fuel for heating is or should be a public responsibility. In addition, we should provide a life-line program for gasoline in order to offset the effect of high prices on the poorer folk who tend to drive older cars with low fuel efficiencies.

5. Broaden the Participation of Citizens in the Formulation of Policy

The government and other groups might well sponsor a program of education. Continuous dialogue involving proposed legislation might be undertaken in from five to ten thousand centers throughout the states. (Sweden had ten thousand groups discussing energy issues.)

These centers might also function to consider other issues. I assume that such an approach would increase political activity.

In summary, then, these are the principles upon which to develop a reasonable political program which embodies care for all people and the environment and husbands resources without calling for a radical reduction in the standard of living:

a. An increase in the efficiency with which we use energy; the elimination of waste.

b. An emphasis upon renewable, nonpolluting resources, especially solar, wind, and biomass, with increased attention to geothermal and ocean thermal gradients.

c. Special conservation of oil and gas by shifting to the production of alcohol from organic materials, from wastes and from fuel farms, and with some increased use of coal.

d. Increasing use of coal, with special attention to the conditions of mining and burning (fluidized bed process use expanded).

e. A very cautious continued use of the light-water reactors now in use or nearing completion; continued experimentation with fusion; elimination of the large investments in the breeder reactor program.

f. Careful attention to the effect of the energy program upon the poorer people of this country and of the world.

g. A recognition that the people together, through the governmental institutions, should determine the broad policy for the provisions of energy. Use of market mechanisms where possible, but no turning over to such mechanisms of the major responsibility for determining what is supplied and how.

A Religious Response to the Energy Issues
—What Churches Might Do

There are numerous communities and networks of people which embody and encourage life styles that are less energy demanding. Churches and church groups have the potential for moving in such directions. The ecological movement attracts persons who seem to want to be part of a different way of being. But in my judgment new directions, if they are to be sustained, require religious commitment and perspective. The conviction that the earth is the Lord's and that everything is created and has a place in the ultimate meaning and purpose of God—in a way that includes but transcends and takes precedence over our own purposes—provides a perspective that brings into question much of what we do in the development of expensive energy- and resource-consuming goods and services. This religious perspective also reinforces a gradual movement toward new ways of relating to each other, in communities or extended families that would embody the following principles, with due allowance for what is possible with different age levels:

a. Everything that is needed and done—education, health, welfare, recreation, work, housing—would take place much more than at present with the same group of people.

b. Sharing with and caring for all members of the community (extended family), would replace exclusive care for one's own blood family or one's own particular family—the so-called nuclear family of wife, husband, and children. Sharing of services and possessions in order to minimize expenditures is encouraged. Training in skills—carpentry, sewing, plumbing, painting, paramedical skills, auto repair, electricity, appliance repair—is part of the education of all. Everyone would have at least one of these skills. Everyone would be encouraged to develop skills which contribute to the care of the community, without expensive gadgets and expensive services.

c. As soon as age permitted, everyone would be involved in a taskforce or a ministry concerned with a major issue: housing, food, energy, jobs, inflation, imperialism, medicine, mental health, welfare, law and the courts, education, recreation, and powerlessness—as experienced by women, or blacks, or browns, or a particular third world nation. Attending to one such issue for the community would be a key part of education. One of the mission tasks might well be the sponsorship of the kind of public forum advocated above.

d. The physical basis for living would be ordered in such a way as to maximize relationships in activities such as eating, working, playing, singing, dancing, celebrating. Concrete opportunities to care for each other thus would be provided. Places for older people and for those with special needs would be included.

e. Formal opportunities would be provided for the discussion of key issues through forums and study/action groups, introduced chiefly, but not always, by members of the group.

f. Expressive activities would be included: music, painting, pottery, drama, dancing, weaving, wood-carving, and so on.

g. The meaning of the community life for politics would be a constant consideration, although, given the forces of our society, there will be, in the foreseeable future, a conflict between such a *way of being* and that supported generally by the prevailing institutions.

h. There would be public funding of alternative education. For strategic reasons one might well advocate issuing certificates that provide money for the schools of one's choice. Such a program would allow the new communities to organize their own education. Of course, one must be aware that such freedom can be used for all kinds of purposes, including segregation by class or race.

VI. Summary

As we are grasped by the reality which was and is present for us in Jesus Christ, we will act more as if the resources of the world, human and nonhuman, are parts of the creation, gifts of God for all of life, present and future; we will use the resources so that all life has access to resources and so that threats to life from pollution effects are minimized. We will use resources with a care and restraint largely unknown in the dominant ethos of the current American way of life.

We will use different kinds of energy, use energy more efficiently, and make our decisions about energy in different ways. We will develop a national program through broader political processes, both to determine what is desirable and to implement the program.

We need to consider decentralizing the energy productive, processing, and distributing process in order to make it more accessible to our understanding and control. The present centralized processes tend to undermine democratic politics.

Underlying the moral and political issues is the religious issue. We have developed a way of being, a way of life, that requires huge amounts of energy to sustain it. Our differentiated, fragmented life style requires much transportation in order to integrate it economically and personally. Our search for meaning, in the face of the meaninglessness of work and living, generally seems to result in huge expenditures of energy, both in travel and in the purchase of things and services, in order to find respite from boredom, isolation, and fragmentation. Religious groups may begin to embody a different way of being in housing, work, recreation, education, and health care that requires less energy and is more joyful and faithful. And thus the energy issue may be a gift that opens the door to life.

Chapter 4:

The Politics of Energy Policy

by Beverly Harrison*

The Requirements of an Adequate Christian Eco-Justice Ethic

The authors of this volume, whatever our differences in discernment of the energy situation, are united in the conviction that the finitude of fossil fuel resources and the values of a high-energy-consumption society pose a fundamental religious and moral challenge to human beings on this planet. We further agree that our theological and moral perspectives now must accommodate the deepened sense of human interdependence which comes into view when we assess ourselves and our societies from an emergent ecological perspective. This ecological perspective has helped us to recognize that we human beings and our societies are an interlocking and interdependent part of a wider environmental system. We no longer perceive nature merely as something inert, "out there," capable of whatever use we may choose to make of it.

The ecologists have taught us that the demands we make upon our natural environment "answer back," and the ecosystem—as the totality of our relationships and interactions with nature through society—responds to our intervention in intricate ways, with consequences uncalculated in the best laid schemes of human historical

* Professor of Christian Ethics, Union Theological Seminary, New York City.

agents.[1] To use a traditional ethical metaphor not usually extended to inanimate or nonhuman entities in earlier moral philosophy, our environment turns out to impose moral *claims* upon us. These claims, if ignored, may dramatically influence our destinies and limit not only our own historical options, but deeply affect the lives of others on this planet and also the prospects of any surviving heirs.

From an ecological perspective, our use of energy is the most dramatic of the many transactions we enter into with the totality of our environment. Painful as it may be to recognize the fact, it is now all too clear that established patterns of energy use have been developed without heeding the consequences of our actions for our own and others' well-being as parts of the wider ecosystem. Our ravenous use of fossil fuel resources is the most dramatic expression of our insensitivity to the limits imposed by a natural environment which now, increasingly, asserts itself as a living part of "our bodies, ourselves."[2]

It is not enough, however, to view the debates about energy policy as a confrontation between those who acknowledge the limits and constraints imposed by the ecosystem and those more confident that further technological breakthroughs will deliver us from such constraints, important as that debate may be. If the controversy about a public energy policy simply expressed this value conflict, there would be reason to hope that eventually (and perhaps sooner rather than later) the human wisdom of a conservation ethic[3] would commend itself to all concerned.

The Need for Social Analysis

Clarification of the theological and moral foundations of the energy issue is but a first step in determining what an optimal public policy in relation to energy might be from a Christian social ethical perspective. One of the serious failures of much ecologically informed discussion of energy ethics has been a tendency to envision a "salvific ethic"[4] without consideration of the actual conditions for, and consequences of, implementing that ethic at the political level, i.e., the level of social policy formation. It is not enough merely to *envisage* an energy ethic adequate to the insights of Christian theological tradition and appropriate to a well-considered sense of our moral obligations. Determining a just *public* policy regarding energy also requires us to analyze the existing social arrangements which are the institutional matrix in which such an energy policy must be formulated. Clear awareness of who gains and who loses from any particular social policy option is too often lacking among the ecologically attuned public, and for that reason, sensitivity to how one gains political support for morally viable social policies is also sometimes ignored. Any energy policy will bear the mark of existing social arrangements and have consequences for the lives of persons which cannot be understood without serious analysis of the political and economic dynamics of the existing social system.

To put the point another way, we must have an analysis which takes account of *power* in an institutional matrix. It is all too easy, from a moral point of view, to envision power exclusively in expressive terms—i.e., as the capacity of persons and groups to realize goals and values, to attain desired social ends. Only when we see that all social policy is forged in an institutional context do we recognize the critical importance of an analysis which views power also in terms of *relations* between persons and especially between groups of persons and between organizational structures.

From a political perspective, power is best understood as a finite resource—a zero-sum quantity—in which not all goals and interests can be accommodated or adequately compromised. In society, some gain their interests at the expense of others. In the social arena, power takes on the character of the capacity to set limits to others' interests. Power enables some to assert their interest over the interests of others. We are political beings in this sense—pursuing our own interests— not merely because we are "fallen" or sinners, but because we live in a finite world where, at least hypothetically, we cannot be sure that even our legitimate and well-considered interests will be accommodated. Politics is the process of seeking the realization of our interests in society; politics is inherent in our existence as finite, or creaturely, social beings.

However, such abstract, theoretical considerations about power and the nature of society do not clarify the major barrier to moving from moral *norms* to determination of a morally adequate public energy *policy*. Since every proposal for social change emerges within a social context, where certain organizations and groups are already in the ascendancy with respect to shaping public policy and deter- mining what interests that policy will serve, a social ethic must take these power realities into account. An adequate analysis in Christian theological perspective must incorporate a *critical* sense of the existing power dynamics that prevent the realization of a just public energy policy.

Justice in a Theological Context

From the standpoint of Christian theological ethics "justice is the first virtue of social institutions."[5] While an adequate case for the normative priority of justice in relationship to any Christian approach to social policy is outside the scope of this essay, it is important to recall that in the context of biblical theology, our commitment to justice is understood as *the* expression of our covenantal relationship to God. The people of God live under a stringent expectation of communal right relationships in which the meaning of justice is discerned particularly by the way the community deals with those who are most marginated, or are not well-placed to defend their own needs and interests.[6] In biblical terms, the righteous community—the one rightly related to God—is the community which expresses its fidelity to God through concern for the least well-off persons and groups. Jesus radicalized and deepened this prophetic theme of justice in praxis and teaching by identifying *his* continuing presence with the presence of those who were especially victimized by society's existing arrangements.[7] A theologically based ethic of eco-justice cannot aim at anything less than a social policy which takes special account of the effects of that policy on those already most disadvantaged in society.

Nor can a theologically grounded sense of justice allow us to rest content with those minimalist understandings of justice sometimes articulated by moralists who define social justice primarily as requiring concern for "treating like cases alike," or for optimizing procedural fairness in society, important as these considerations are.[8] Rather, the biblical sense of justice focuses on actual human need. Biblical justice requires direct address to real, lived inequities, and critical scrutiny of and protest against institutional arrangements which pervasively perpetuate and deepen social inequities. No Christian ethical analysis can avoid facing the politics of energy policy nor overlook the deep-seated barriers which block the way to a radical, relationally inclusive standard of social justice in the production and use of energy resources.

The Depth of the Problem as Exhibited in the National Energy Debate

Much that has occurred in the initial process of developing a national energy policy for the United States illustrates the difficulty of surfacing fundamental questions of justice in public policy debate. It should be recalled that neither corporate energy producers nor those who perceive their interests to be very different opposed

President Carter's effort to develop a national energy policy. This fact might be considered surprising in a nation where most business interests and a sizable sector of the public espouse a social philosophy that the least government is the best government. But a superficial consensus about the need for a national energy policy masks the fact that there is little agreement as to the nature of the energy crisis. Few are prepared, even now, to discern how deeply divided we are as a people on the question.

One of the reasons why none objected to the development of a federal policy is that the federal gomernment has long been involved in energy policy in several important ways: (a) at the regulatory level;[9] (b) in providing tax incentives which have shaped the previous course of energy development;[10] and (c) in massive direct support for research and development of certain lines of energy supply, most especially in relation to developing nuclear power.[11] Because the government is already deeply involved, no one on any side of the energy debate could plausibly argue that it was in the national interest for the government to take a more passive role. Moreover, in face of mounting evidence that ad hoc approaches to energy policy could result in dislocation of energy supply, with severe repercussions to the economy and increased political tensions domestically or internationally, no serious argument against a national energy policy was possible. The important point, however, is that all sides in the public policy debate recognized that formation of a more coherent national public policy held out promise of shaping that policy in a way congenial to their long-term interests. From the outset, then, a wide range of conflicting interests *converged* to support the momentum for national policy.

In his initial appeals for public support for the development of the national policy, President Carter especially stressed the need to recognize the dangers of profligate use of limited fossil fuel resources, and tried to heighten public awareness of the dangers to our national security of extreme dependence upon imported oil. Out of this analysis he identified as primary goals of his program *conservation* of energy resources and *production shifts* that would increase our independence of foreign sources of supply. In addition, he pledged *fairness* in distributing the costs and hardships of the policy as a basic goal. Nearly twenty months later, Congress enacted an energy package which does not reflect in any adequate way these originally stated presidential goals and priorities. And the American people are, it is widely reported, more confused than before about the nature of the energy crisis. The degree of confusion among the general public as to the nature of "the crisis" is a sure sign that the superficial consensus on the need for a national policy obscured more than it revealed.

The Power Monopoly

The national energy policy debate dramatically illustrated the inordinate existing disparities of power (in the zero-sum sense) which operated in the formation of the present energy policy. With the immense power of corporate energy producers arrayed against him, President Carter and his major energy policy advisers conceded at the outset that the chief strategy in curbing energy (particularly oil) consumption would be use of market pricing mechanisms, with tax write-off incentives as a second strategy for encouraging conservation and redistributing costs of the policy. A third policy option, the use of direct grants to lighten the cost burden on certain segments of the population and to encourage more rapid shifts toward renewable energy sources, was not envisioned as a major strategy because of pressures against "inflationary" governmental expenditures.

As a candidate for the presidency, Carter had said some brave things about the massive power of the major oil corporations and had spoken sympathetically of the need for governmental action to curtail their monopoly power and to restore freer market conditions, so that the public would not pay excessively for its energy supply. Carter did not endorse *vertical* divestiture—the effort to limit corporate control to one of several stages of the oil production process, i.e., extraction, refining, transportation or marketing of oil. But he had supported *horizontal* divestiture, or the effort to prevent the trend toward monopoly control by a few corporations of production of different types of energy—oil, coal, nuclear power, and so on. This would have meant an effort to curb the accelerating expansion of the major oil corporations into production of other forms of energy.[12]

By the time the president unveiled his initial energy proposals, he had backed away from any initiatives in the direction of horizontal divestiture. This decision not to take any action in restraint of growing concentration in the energy production field, combined with the decision made at the outset of the debate to rely on pricing and tax-incentive mechanisms to implement an energy policy, meant that the executive branch was unwilling to mount serious pressure to offset the massive power of energy producers, whose interests are always well protected in Congress.

The new energy legislation does authorize a closer monitoring of the financial operations of the energy producers, but those who know the history of previous efforts to monitor the activities of the oil corporations cannot be optimistic about these new efforts.[13] In fact, given the weakness of control mechanisms written into the national energy legislation or mandated by it, there is every reason to doubt that the new energy policy will inhibit expansionist dynamics toward monopoly control of energy production. And because the National Energy Act of 1978 drastically centralizes governmental decision-making and administration of government policy, public oversight of governmental monitoring activities in this area may in fact become more difficult.[14] The entire congressional debate largely ignored the well-documented reality of monopoly power in energy production.[15] The only critical questions were asked by a coalition of "consumer advocates" in the House and Senate and their efforts focused on a losing struggle to extract some compromises on energy pricing mechanisms, especially in the area of natural gas production.[16]

The Producers' Interpretation

During the entire period of debate on the legislation, the American people were treated to an unprecedented campaign of propaganda initiated by energy producers. Through television advertising and the print media we were subjected to unrelenting industry "interpretation" of the energy crisis. Mobil Oil and other major oil companies became the main educators as to the nature of the crisis. The spectacle of the most powerful interested parties in the national policy debate spending large sums from the vast corporate resources at their command to shape public opinion, under the guise of presenting the only "economically sound" approach, raises the question whether points of view other than those of the multinational corporation will ever again get equal time in national public policy discussions.[17] Small wonder that the American people are said to be more confused than ever about the character of the energy crisis. The corporate line, as exhibited in the Mobil pedagogy, was bound to confuse. For example, the public was informed that our high energy consumption is due to the government's previous efforts at price regulation! We were told that because our political leaders had opted for "popular" solutions such as price regulation in the past, we had indulged ourselves in natural gas usage. These misguided regulatory efforts, we were assured, had been made "in ... the guise of helping the consumer, punishing certain 'villains,' or providing an instant 'answer' to a pressing problem...."[18]

The oil industries' "solution" for achieving the needed conservation of energy (this stress on conservation was a new value in the

Pandora's box of corporate "concerns") was, of course, return to what Mobil called "free market" pricing mechanisms—i.e., leaving pricing to the corporate producers. By invoking appeal to a purported "free market" dear to the value systems of many Americans who have little technical understanding of the massively monopolistic conditions currently existing in the energy field, the industry was clearly attempting to dispel widespread suspicion about the role of the corporations in accelerating the rise of oil and gas prices. Mobil warned the public, in soberest terms, that such free market conditions, while encouraging a climate of conservation, would not be sufficient to avert a crisis. If our "total environment"—by which Mobil meant our present standard of living—was to be maintained, we must rapidly increase the production of alternative fuels—gas, shale, and nuclear energy.[19] Not surprisingly, these are the alternative energy sources in which oil companies have already made major investments, and where incursions of oil corporation capital have been heavily centered. Mobil shied away from direct attack on environmental interest groups by lumping environmentalists with those who seek "popular" and "short-term" solutions.[20] They also acknowledged the probable *eventual* importance of solar, geothermal and other renewable energy sources, thereby projecting an open image while offering comforting assurance that we could solve this real and genuine crisis with a minimum of social dislocation and discomfort. What serious and long-term students of the major oil corporations have come to call "the private government of energy" so thoroughly controlled the processes of information flow to the public and causal interpretation of the energy crisis during the period of congressional debate on energy policy that public awareness of corporate monopoly of energy production seems less vivid today than ever before.

We ended the first round of development of a national energy policy, then, with the most powerful of the interested parties in the debate unscathed, and with even greater likelihood of increasing concentrations of power in energy production and supply. A few major corporations will continue to have the major voice in the future course of energy policy unless the public comes to understand the problem more clearly and to act accordingly. Public sensitivity to the negative consequences of this state of affairs will probably be further undermined by continuance of corporate "educational" efforts.

The entire congressional debate was, as noted, cast as a confrontation between the interests of producers and consumers—with all lines converging on one or the other side of the way interests are construed by the advanced capitalist market model. Any compromises between the interests of the corporations and interests of those who construe the common welfare differently than the corporations are mediated through the categories established by the market system. Concessions to "consumers" may be made, especially as politicians face impending elections, but concerns for our common and personal well-being which do not fit the dynamics of existing patterns of production and consumption in the market may enter less and less into discussion. Insofar as the "public interest" has been reduced to "consumer concerns," there will be even less room for the substantive questions of social justice in the on-going process of shaping and implementing energy policy.

The Least Well-Off Are the Ongoing Losers

To construe the American public merely as an abstract collection of *consumers* who are assumed to have nothing more at stake in energy policy than concern for pressure on their pocketbooks is worrisome enough. It means that our national energy policy tends less and less to take account of how that policy affects already existing inequities in the American economic system. But equally, construing the *interests* at stake in the political process in this way will make it increasingly difficult to focus upon how United States policy affects inequities between our nation and other nations, especially those nations which are currently disadvantaged in terms of the dynamics of the global economic system.

While the questions about a just energy policy on a global scale are too complex to be treated in this essay, we do need to note that existing patterns of inequity between nations are reinforced and deepened by the energy crisis. In this respect, the power dynamics of the world market system repeat themselves globally, as they do at home; however, poor nations have even less power in policy tradeoffs than do the disadvantaged in the United States. For those of us who are citizens of the rich advanced industrial nations, all of our productive activities, including those aimed at our fundamental survival needs (food, shelter, clothing), and those aimed at enhancing the quality of our lives, and those which are mere luxuries,[21] involve the high consumption of energy. The poorest nations are those where increased energy resources are needed even to begin to meet the survival needs of people.

The world market system is such that our globe is divided roughly between advanced industrial systems with diversified economies, whose world market exports include a range of goods and who have excess manufactured goods to sell abroad, and those nations whose economic systems are not so diversified, and whose major source of capital in world trade is the sale of their natural resources, which must be sold at often low commodity prices in order to buy other natural resources and manufactured goods which they do not produce. Manufactured goods are extremely costly in relation to the prices these nations receive for their own commodities. This global class system has been intensified because high world market prices for energy have devoured the meager resources of the market-disadvantaged nations, and made capital formation for economic development even harder. Efforts to address the basic survival needs of their people have been set back, and even nations which have no wish to duplicate the questionable patterns of "economic development" of the advanced industrial systems have been forced into greater dependency on the rich nations, with attendant loss of political autonomy, and have had to open their doors to foreign corporate capital that deeply skews their development away from economic policies which give priority to the survival needs of their people. The only exception to this state of affairs is the cartel of oil-producing nations, who have been able to accelerate capital formation due to the rising demand for oil. But most of the nations in the world do not have sufficient natural resources or capacity for capital formation to allow them to avoid a downward poverty spiral as the energy crisis worsens. Only fundamental changes in the global economic order and a loosening pressure on fossil fuel consumption in the industrial nations can help them.

This is why conservation and shifts away from fossil fuel consumption in the rich world are so urgent morally. The problem is exacerbated by the fact that until now the only alternative form of energy to fossil fuels given priority by industrial nations has been the development of nuclear power. Increasingly, as evidence mounts that reliance on these forms of nuclear energy will have disastrous consequences ecologically, and as it becomes clearer that the social and economic costs of a plutonium economy are staggering, the nuclear solution is being rejected by citizens of the advanced industrial societies. Still, their governments (including our own) continue to expend vast sums in support of this industry. Meanwhile, alternative energy supplies from renewable sources are given less than central priority in the energy policies of the rich nations. All of this increases the numbers of countries which are *being made poor*.

Similar dynamics repeat themselves at the domestic level. President Carter's original goal to distribute the added costs of energy policy fairly was both good politics and good morality. The public is unlikely to support any policy it feels requires sacrifices not well distributed in the society. The problem, however, is that even without the energy crisis, the economic situation of most people in American society is worsening. And ours is a society where the deep economic disparities which exist are mystified and not well understood. Because of our *collective* affluence, and because disparities of economic wealth are less apparent in a society where the vast majority of people have access to survival needs—food, shelter, and clothing—most of us fail to realize that the total economic wealth of our nation is distributed as unevenly as is the wealth of a nation such as India.[22] Furthermore, our ideology of success, and the notion that the United States is a society in which effort and merit are rewarded, works against persons acknowledging and protesting their disadvantaged economic position in this society.[23]

It has long been recognized that at least one-fifth of our population exists as a poverty subculture, outside direct participation in the productive economy.[24] Nonwhite Americans, women, the elderly and handicapped, and persons living in economically underdeveloped regions of the country, are all dramatically overrepresented in this subculture in proportion to their numbers in society at large.[25] In addition, as our population grows older, this subculture will grow even if (as is doubtful) unemployment rates drop for other reasons. *Unemployment* is not likely to decrease without large increases in the economic growth rate, because our high-technology economy and our technologically oriented modes of production are yielding fewer and fewer jobs in the productive center of the economy, in proportion to the number of persons who need work in the society as a whole.

We are witnessing a growing differentiation between skilled and unskilled labor. While the wages of skilled labor in the private sector of the economy may increase in some rough relation to increasing living costs—due to the fact that organized labor is most effective in protecting the position of those who are skilled—the real wages of unskilled workers will not do so. Where jobs are funded by taxes, and this includes workers who deliver services funded by government at all levels, we are likely to see large cutbacks and heavy pressure for wage restraints which will move many workers to lower positions on the income spectrum. Persons who are newly entering the job market are finding that the work most readily available is in the less skilled and lower-paying end of the job spectrum, or in parts of the country where organized labor is weak and in no position to provide pressure against wage restraints. Competition for access to high-income work—especially professional and professional-managerial positions[26]—is growing more intense as students are warned away from the middle-income service positions funded through the public sector of the economy, especially teaching, social work and the like.

These shifts are the structural basis for the economic pressures now being experienced by the great majority of Americans. *Inflation*, which usually gets the blame for the misery many are experiencing, is not really an independent economic variable. Rather it is both a cause and an effect of all these shifting economic patterns, including, of course, the high costs of energy[27] and the high level of "costs" energy producers charge against profit levels for "research, development, and capital expansion." The high level of loss of real income which so many citizens are experiencing slowed but finally did not deter the president's plans to effect energy conservation through pricing mechanisms. And it was a purported threat of a taxpayers' revolt which served as a check upon more extensive use of direct grants to shape energy policy in desirable ways. Monies to be spent on direct grants through the Energy Act of 1978 are extremely small, too small to have much effect on redistributing the costs of the new energy policy or in encouraging genuine conservation. Loan funds for the middle-income elderly fared better in Congress than did direct grant proposals. But in the end, only tax-credit strategies were widely used, and most of the tax-credit benefits went to business rather than directly to the public.

The problem with tax incentives is that they work, if at all, only for those who are now at least moderately affluent. Low-interest loans expand the social base of tax-incentive programs and increase the numbers of those who can take advantage of tax provisions, but one must have a margin of resources above survival needs to benefit from such loans. Even though increased energy costs are reflected in rising prices at every level, these increases most affect those whose income and financial resources stretch only to cover basic survival needs.

An adequate assessment of how much more drastically the poor, including not only those outside the productive economy but also millions of working poor, are affected by the costs of energy use is not possible here. The seriousness of the situation can be illustrated, though, by noting what rising home fuel costs have done to citizens classified as poor by official government standards. In 1976, middle-income families were spending 4 to 7 percent of their incomes for such fuel. By comparison, low-income households were using only half as much electricity and a quarter less natural gas than were middle-income families, but this smaller usage cost between 15 and

25 percent of the total income of these families. Recent commentators contend that in some areas 30 to 50 percent of total income of poor families goes to such fuel expenditures.[28] Obviously, for such persons, belt tightening does not mean foregoing luxuries or enhancement needs. It means cutting essentials such as food and clothing. In this context it is easy to see why tax incentives are not so beneficial to those least advantaged. Poor people do not have the capital to pay for conservation measures in the first place, and loans, even low-interest loans, are just as irrelevant, since they could not repay them. Because the primary relief mechanisms of energy policy implementation cannot work for them, the poor pay most for our energy policy.

The new energy policy also distributes costs inequitably in the direction of the poor and lower-middle-income groups at several other important points. In a society without adequate public transportation and addicted to the automobile culture, lower-income persons, especially the working poor, expend a higher percentage of their incomes for transportation than do those who earn more. Many persons in our society simply must have automobiles if they are to work at all, since alternative transportation frequently is not available, and the best jobs are often located at some distance from centers of population, or in areas where housing costs are high. The National Energy Policy Act of 1978 makes little effort to wean us from our dependency on the automobile; national transportation policy has yet to be coordinated with energy policy.[29] The Energy Act does impose some tax penalties on persons who insist upon purchasing gas-guzzling automobiles, but the cost of gasoline is sure to increase and those who need the automobile to stay in the job market will be hardest hit. Nor can the working poor always avoid gas guzzlers, since they must often buy cheaper second-hand vehicles, which are very fuel-inefficient. Those who have discretionary income for luxuries (and who are the major proportionate consumers of gasoline in any case) may not be much deterred by higher gasoline prices and taxes on fuel-inefficient cars in any case. But those who use the automobile chiefly for access to jobs and for related survival needs will be hard hit indeed.

Only the *most* well-off in this society can afford to disregard the consequences of energy policy in two other important areas of human well-being—its impact on creating jobs and its consequences in terms of human health. Here low- and middle-income Americans can find common ground in support of policies which serve their mutual interest. But in order to appreciate why there is so much common ground in terms of what is good for poor and middle strata people in this society, we must help people to understand how misleading are the energy industry's projected scenarios of what is at stake in these areas.

The unemployment threat argument has been perhaps the most powerful factor in the federal government's repeated acquiescence to corporation ideology in many areas of public policy, and the politics of energy policy has been no exception. Until recently, many took at face value the energy producers' claims that any shift in existing priorities for new energy production from nuclear power would result in escalating unemployment and economic dislocations. This claim is still believed, despite mounting evidence compiled by public interest groups, showing that the energy policies which would best address our unemployment ills are those which are most benign in terms of health and safety. Serious conservation efforts would create new jobs, as would the rapid development of a decentralized solar industry and the development of other renewable energy sources.[30] The jobs created by such policy options would be scattered across the country rather than located at energy boom sites, as with fossil fuel extraction jobs or nuclear power-related positions. Many energy boom sites, including those that will be created by increased reliance on coal and shale, are located in what are now sparsely populated areas, so the social costs of these developments must be recognized to include the costs of building new communities—i.e., expanding services for boom towns—and the costs of moving workers and their families to such sites. Nuclear power, a high-technology industry, produces relatively few jobs in relation to the massive capital expenditures required for its development. And the use of nuclear power and coal carries the hidden social costs of serious health hazards to employees and to the public, especially those who live near extraction or production locations.[31]

No one can precisely assess the indirect costs nor the wider environmental damage which will occur from reliance upon high-technology energy production, but there is no doubt that industry projections of the costs of energy production include few of these. It is time we learned that such social costs will be paid, not by the industry involved, but by citizens, who will shoulder the price of remedial government services to victims or of most environmental reclamation which occurs. For example, the estimated minimum cost to taxpayers for cleaning up the West Valley Nuclear Waste storage site in upstate New York is $600,000,000. The administration's energy package gives little evidence that such costs and inequities have been weighed in the formation of public policy. Some hard-won environmental restrictions have been maintained, but discretionary governmental regulatory powers may erode these in the future. The relative inaction and noninvolvement of the departments of Labor and Health, Education and Welfare in formulation of the national energy plan[32] are troublesome indicators of how far we have to go in measuring who gains and who loses in energy policy. Fortunately, though, coalitions of persons and groups deeply concerned about the effects of a national energy policy on jobs and health are beginning to challenge the conventional data generated by and propounded through industry, which result in largely misplaced fears that a sound energy policy will have detrimental consequences for the total economy.

Conclusion

Two years of "the politics of energy" should not allow us to be at ease about the adequacy of our policies in light of fundamental standards of social justice. In spite of massive and growing grass-roots activity aimed at shaping energy policy in a humane direction—one that recognizes the interconnections between the quality of life and fairness—little has been accomplished at the national level. We have no option but to work to increase the public's growing sophistication about what a just social policy would look like, and this effort must be made in face of massive "educational" efforts by those who will claim that our ecojustice perspectives are "utopian" and dangerous. Too much is at stake for all of us—including future generations whose interests can only be represented through the moral adequacy of the policies which we now adopt—to allow us to abandon efforts at developing public momentum for an energy policy which really represents the *public* interest. As Christians we have no choice but to accelerate our involvement, working together with coalitions of persons who are engaged in these concerns.[33]

Our churches must become centers for reexamining our personal and institutional values and lifestyles, but must also become places where countereducation on energy *policy* questions can occur. We must give wide hearing to public interest groups who are generating data which challenges the conventional wisdom of the energy-producing corporations. Otherwise, the public debate will continue to be thrashed out within parameters that cut off or ignore much needed information. Most importantly, we must speak out and act politically to press the claims of the least well-off in society, pointing to the growing disparities of wealth and privilege. We must also call our government to account for its persistent failure to address the seriousness of the global crisis of inequities between rich and poor nations. Unless these deepening inequities are reversed, the privileged minority will continue to undermine the very conditions of human survival on this planet. In societies and between nations riddled with social inequities, the rich themselves can only survive by turning their world into an armed camp in which privilege prevails, if it does, for a while through the barrel of a gun.

Chapter 5:

Ways to Influence Energy Systems

by Douglas Still*

Introduction: Sun Day—A Model

On the first national celebration of Sun Day, May 3, 1978, tens of millions of people from widely diversified economic and political backgrounds joined together to assert that an energy revolution must begin to occur in our collective experience.

Motives

Many millions of people participated in Sun Day because of public interest and private moral revulsion over our extravagant use of fossil fuels. They took seriously the kind of data provided by R. Buckminster Fuller's testimony to a United States Senate subcommittee: "We are not justified in using the energy savings account of fossil fuels where the energy-hour investment in their creation and storage would cost us today possibly as much as one billion dollars a gallon, figured at present kilowatt-hour generating rates."[1] These fossil fuels are selling at about one dollar a gallon for gasoline. They are being used up for frivolous purposes and will last a bare thirty to forty more years before they are completely expended at the present rate of consumption. "Soft" energy production is the logical alter-

*Oregon field organizer for the Center for Environmental Action

native, if fossil fuels are to be conserved and remain available to meet essential needs of our children and children's children.

Many people participated in Sun Day out of technical interest in the mechanics of capturing and using solar energy for water and space heating, electric generation, and propulsion of vehicles.

Many participated because of the excitement of parades, musical events, radio and television coverage, and thereby developed a curiosity about how solar energy works.

Some representatives of organized labor participated because they believed that solar energy developments will offer a wide spectrum of new employment possibilities for organized labor.

Some utility company personnel participated because of anxiety and frustration that this field of energy development does not lend itself easily to centralized corporate control, and the belief that widespread individual investments in solar power will potentially reduce future utility corporation profits. Significant efforts were therefore exerted in many areas, by utilities, to coopt planning for Sun Day.

Many solar energy advocates and those personally committed to life styles oriented to "appropriate technology" participated in hopes of finding future employment in solar-oriented citizen action groups.

Hundreds of other motives of participants can be imagined. Probably everyone had a combination of altruistic and personal interest motives prompting their interest in and support of Sun Day.

Objectives

Sun Day was an energy organizing event bent on achieving two goals: 1) to demonstrate a broad, popular, public appreciation of the immense energy potential of solar resources *if* they were only economically and politically structured to come into full development; and 2) to send a message to a reticent and timid national political administration that (a) the public is far better informed about environmentally benign energy alternatives than elected officials believe, and (b) that they had better shift some of our national energy priorities in the direction of solar energy systems.

It would appear that the message, in part, got through! President Carter took immediate action to increase the solar budget of USDOE by $100 million! But celebrations, even on the national level of citizen organization, do not have much direct potential impact on the shape or direction of energy policies. Like Earth Day before it, Sun Day will prove to have been a significant event *if* it serves as a springboard for major local, state, and national efforts to give a changed focus to hundreds of legislative policy decisions, administrative appointments, and budget allocations. Solar policy decisions will also be made by public utility commissions, energy facility siting councils, TVAs (Tennessee Valley Authority), BPAs (Bonneville Power Administration), etc. In other words, if citizens are not active in their demand for accurate information and timely consultation when energy decisions are made, and if citizens do not demand accountability of utility executives to the public interest, then Sun Day and similar events remain symbolic. Only citizens' groups that bird-dog legislative processes and energy administration agencies can expect to achieve energy policy changes that reflect Sun Day values. In this respect, it is encouraging to note the very high level of citizen sophistication among Sun Day coalitions. Earth Day was a watershed for national environmental legislation, and Sun Day, hopefully, will be a watershed for changed energy policies.

Sun Day is an example of coalitional politics on the national level in which the churches have joined with other segments of society to impact public policy decision-making. The National Council of Churches joined with the United Auto Workers, the Sierra Club, Friends of the Earth, Environmental Action, the Machinists Union, the Solar Energy Industry Association, and dozens of other national organizations to transmute citizen interest into citizen power through political mobilization for change in energy priorities. With relatively minor financial investment, but with major time and human energy allocations (Sun Day was labor-intensive), a significant event occurred which may have far-reaching public policy consequences.

Strategies for Change

A. Some Organizing First Principles

1. People Power

Citizen altruism and good intentions are ethereal and usually expressed primarily in sermons and on baccalaureate occasions. They are undependable as a basis for organizing citizen action. Covering over citizen grievances and community hostilities is always the goal of the privileged and the oppressors. It is the primary talent of successful politicians and administrators. Justice is the goal of the "outs," and those *seeking* to be "in." In the political process, there can be no reconciliation between the ins and the outs unless the reason for hostility or unequal distribution of benefits is clarified, defined, and articulated to all parties related to a conflict situation.

Peace is sought by bringing parties to a conflict into negotiation. The strong and powerful seldom want peace; they want continued dominance over their sphere of influence. When the *influence* or the *power* of different groups in conflict is widely spread, the group with large power is seldom inclined to recognize the claims for accommodation by the weak group. It is incumbent for the cause of justice for public policy to seek to equalize the power of groups in conflict. This is the conventional course of reconciliation/peace. To allow rival claimants to remain unequal in power leads frequently to strategies of violence by the group which remains unrecognized—that is, powerless. It appears to be the case that the degree of violence in a society is a measure of the injustice of that society. It is more than happenstance that the United States is one of the most violence-prone social scenes in the civilized world. The everlasting problem of peace at home, or abroad, is the problem of getting or forcing the strong to allow the increase of power by the poor or weak.

2. Money

For social change organizations to have continuity and influence, they must have victories in achieving their objectives. Social change victories are not easily achieved; but they are far from uncommon in the history of American social policy. If the churches are serious in the effort to achieve change in social, political or economic policy, they must be realistic about the requirements for organizational success in achieving change.

There has been far too much rhetoric on the part of the churches that they are committed to change, and far too little hard evidence that they are, in fact, serious about their commitment. If the churches are serious about energy policy change, one of the primary means to succeed—money—must be provided to compatible social change organizations, either alone or in coalition with other groups.

Two essential ingredients for effective social change strategy are the availability of skilled, experienced community organizers on the one hand, and a source of funding for organizational efforts which is sufficient to achieve defined objectives.

Needless to say, unless there are dedicated, effective, local citizen volunteers ready to give leadership, none of the above can be implemented.

3. Personnel

The trained organizer will always have an intimate, sensitive knowledge of who and what his or her constituency is: i.e., its size, range of interests, motives, its leadership (with all its strengths, weaknesses, and the dynamics of competition for leadership change). The organizer will understand, and have clearly detailed within the organization, its goals, long- and short-term objectives, and a clear understanding of the probable responses of the group when challenged to take action. He will understand objectives and processes which will captivate the interest and excitement of the membership.

The organizer will help the leadership of the organization know what the blocks to goal achievement are. He/she will help the group to personify these blocks, i.e., to identify an enemy(ies). Simplifying issues for easy description is very important. The leadership will know the needs, interests, priorities, strengths and weaknesses of the opposition. In order to have victories, the community organizer and the leadership will analyze the power structure. They will determine achievable aims on the road to full goal achievement by the organization. They will assess the range of possible reactions of the opposition to any action the organization takes. It is in the subsequent action of the organization, to the reaction of the opposition, that success or failure of the organization's tactic will be measured. Therefore, a full range of strategic ideas for action has to be carefully reviewed by all the citizens' organizational leadership, prior to the initiation of any strategy for change.

It is clear that these strategic plans must simultaneously catch the enemy off-guard and be an occasion for fun by and with the organization's membership. The opposition may be quite heavy-handed in its response, giving the organization a public relations windfall. But occasionally the opposition's response is designed to offer no more than a long, protracted period of nonnews, during which a sophisticated opposition will seek to coopt the citizen leadership of the organization. Such possibilities need to be planned for and avoided, or counteracted by another action. The organization will obviously need cooperative allies who provide legal and strategic counsel, support of ordinances or legal authority, or a citizen mandate impelling the opposition to some action or change. Governmental agency staff support and police understanding (or at least neutrality) are necessary, and financial security during a period of crucial confrontation is essential. Capacity to provide press services to the media is also essential. Do not assume that a sympathetic press will be available. The media usually "belong" to the established order, especially to high-spending advertisers, like utilities. Citizen action must often overcome a hostile press and media.

If negotiation between the parties is undertaken, some intermediate victories should be sought, and effected, as the negotiations proceed. It is absolutely essential that, as resolution of one issue or achievement of a particular victory is in hand, the planning proceed for the defining and organizing necessary to move to the next achievable goal for the organization.

4. Hot to Cold Anger

A word needs to be said about the way in which anger and enthusiasm are dealt with in citizen organizing. The grievances and frustrations of citizens are the bread and butter of organizational life. Without them, there is no oomph or punch to sustain organizational dynamic. The importance of rage cannot be minimized! Grievances and righteous indignation need to be articulated, and the resulting grievance resolution process is the purpose of the organization. The heightening of frustration may very well be a major need in getting citizens into an organizing frame of mind. At the same time, it is very clear that hot anger must be turned into cold, controlled strategy if victories are to be achieved.

The leadership in the life of an organization must not lose passion for the cause. But passion is going to be expressed in action with care and high deliberation. The opposition may be made to look as selfish and stupid as possible—but in such action one's organization must take care to keep the self-interest of its members protected. To be wrong is forgivable; to be stupid is not. And to let hot anger direct action is to court strategic stupidity. The opposition deserves careful study and a choice of strategy and tactics that are legitimate in the eyes of the action organization.

B. Energy Organizing

What do these general organizing principles mean in the field of energy policy? Citizens who are apt to become organized for energy policy change reflect a wide gamut of concerns. Among those who can be easily organized on a self-interest basis are the following:

1. The membership of environmental organizations reads widely about the threats to community survival and planetary survival that are represented by the pellmell rush of the energy companies to grow, grow, grow. In Oregon, for example, people talk about avoiding californication: growth at *any* cost, which is perceived as typical of the California decision makers. Environmentally oriented people are already motivated to struggle for maintenance of high community

standards and are therefore usually easily organized, and their organizations usually make good participants in coalitional organization
efforts, though they seldom have any money.

2. Large numbers of the privileged segment of society closely
follow health and nutrition news. These people are easily aroused
when utility and government executives try to soft-peddle their new
plants on a benefit/risk argument basis. Most informed people are
now very suspicious of the mathematical ratios served up by the
profit-minded corporate leadership and their closely allied public
agency friends. The number of people alarmed by the rapid growth
of cancer, lung, and heart diseases among the population at large
want to prevent unnecessary industrial and residential developments
which will impair the quality of air, water, and the environment. The
carcinogenic and debilitative poisons must be reduced, not increased.
The people who are informed about health and nutrition matters are
concerned to prevent huge increases in energy consumption.

3. The readership of *Prevention Magazine* or *Mother Jones* and a
vast array of similar contemporary periodical literature, and those
who read E.F. Schumacher's *Small Is Beautiful* or are influenced by
Barry Commoner in writings like *Poverty of Power*, are people in
affluent homes. Often their teenage and college-age youth are exploring alternative life styles. The very high public interest in "appropriate technology" reaches from high school science classes to the
White House. This is a segment of the population that understands
the ethic of resource husbandry and the principle that "there is no
such thing as a free lunch." Given the opportunity to shape public
policies which effectively reflect that ethic, they will welcome appropriate energy policy changes to maintain the planet and their locale
as a good place to rear their families.

4. Mechanization on the docks, in trucking, shipping, agriculture,
retail marketing, construction trades, and in every other field of
economic activity has led to widespread unemployment, and thousands of the employed are insecure because they see their jobs being
automated out of existence. Increasing numbers of people are experiencing the reality that our economic system seems almost mindless
to the need for fruitful and meaningful work—both for a sense of
significance and for income. Most of the scenarios for vastly increasing large-scale energy-generating plants promise progress of the type
we have experienced in the past—more new high-technology jobs for
a relatively few energy priests of a new order. These energy scenarios
also promise more leisure for the well-to-do, and the optimists of
these scenarios would assert a trickle-down benefit for the poor. But

large segments of the public and their public-interest organizational leadership discern that the types of employment left over are subservient, powerless, low-paying jobs in service industries.

Modes of energy development can be pursued which offer more jobs and more employment for more people across a more widely scattered range of communities, which reverse the centralization of power and tend to return control of capital, plant, and jobs to the local scene. Those labor and community leaders acquainted with the promises of these rival energy scenarios are high potential leaders and participants in energy change organizations.

5. For people living on retirement and fixed incomes, and for those who choose life styles which do not benefit from the inflationary spirals of the growth of the new technology, the steeply rising costs of utility bills are a threat to survival itself. Not all of these people think of themselves as "outs." They have been the "ins" of the past—but they observe themselves being pushed into poverty by fast-buck, fast-growth community leaders.

6. Large numbers of people in the nation live in communities and pursue livelihoods which are being overwhelmed by vast new water, land, and air requirements of the huge new nuclear and coal plants. All of the following are impacting peoples' lives in new ways: long-distance pipelines; high-tension transmission systems; coal slurry pipelines moving scarce water from one watershed to another; farm lands subject to coal and uranium surface mining; air shed regions vastly deteriorated by plant stack pollution; valleys to be inundated by new dams; communities to serve as hosts for new, dangerous, industrial waste disposal systems; fishing communities threatened by installation of oil refining plants; or villages threatened by installation of potentially high-hazard, liquid natural gas reservoirs; and many others. It is far too often the case that citizens only hear about such expropriation of their environment after the fact. Given forewarning, people in such places are good prospects for participation in energy change organizations. If organizing occurs *after* plant siting decisions, the range of organizing options is more limited, but the number of angry people willing to participate is probably far larger!

7. A few people in our society will participate in political change activity from the primary motivation of reason, knowledge, and principle. However, do not look to the universities and schools of higher education for leadership or assistance. With only few exceptions, the residents of academia are nonparticipants in vital change activity related to community well-being. The professors are busy doing "research" for the energy companies, or for other established

power order groups and organizations. Exceptions to this observation may not stay very long. The power and reach of the energy companies have all but emasculated the theory of scientific objectivity, or of academic freedom, in our technical schools. Scientific objectivity has been compromised by the dominance of research grants and special study research projects which are supported by industry and government. Where academic leaders do identify with a citizens' organization whose views are not conventional, they face sniping by peers. Citizen groups and leaders should not be intimidated by "experts." Just publicize the list of donors of the grants under which they work!

C. Blocks to Change in the Energy Marketplace

1. Centralized Control

There are many genuinely powerful leaders on the state and national level who wish they had the power to be influential in relation to the centralized control of the major oil and utility companies. Not many can claim that influence! Should the average citizen have any confidence that *we* can help shape energy policy? By ourselves, we are almost impotent. But in concert, citizens can effect major changes in policy when they ally themselves in coalition with other public-spirited groups whose interests parallel the change desired. Muscle is developed in democratic organizational enterprise. It requires that organizational leadership have clear intentions, careful investment of personal energy, and astute assessment of the ups and downs in the dynamics and debates of current issues.

2. Timing Constraints

Timing is crucial for success. For this reason citizen movements usually limit themselves to only a few possible objectives for change at any one time. This requires of citizen groups an open-mindedness and a relative flexibility of focus on particulars, as they seek to change a major aspect of the economic system.

3. Ideological Leadership

Groups whose common interest is rooted in a narrow political or economic ideological framework seldom give effective leadership to citizen coalition efforts. This is because, to be successful, such efforts need to attract a wide range of citizen interest and commitment which span various political philosophies and dogmas. Also, citizens are highly skeptical of the true motives of narrowly ideological leaders when these persons propose to lead coalition movements. To succeed, leadership must be accepted as in the middle range of the spectrum of democratic political values.

4. Power Structure

To have strategic success, any organizational movement, whether on the local, state, or national level, must carefully and accurately assess where power for decision lies. In relation to energy systems, this tends to be highly centralized. Most people are aware that decision-making power in the oil industry is highly concentrated, but most do not realize that the same holds true in the electric utility industry. In the United States, 77 percent of our electricity comes from about two hundred investor-owned utilities (IOUs); the other 23 percent comes from over three thousand publicly-owned systems— many of which buy their energy from the IOUs. The federal government generates about 12 percent of the nation's power through agencies like the TVA (the Tennessee Valley Authority) or BPA (the Bonneville Power Administration), but it has no retail customers.[2]

Moreover, a relatively few large banks control large blocks of the voting stock of the two hundred largest IOUs. The personnel who exercise influence over the trust departments of these banks are frequently directors of the utilities themselves. Thus is the power of control over the electric utility industry highly centralized!

Furthermore, the energy companies are increasingly spreading their interests over the whole spectrum of energy resources. For instance, oil companies control large segments of the uranium industry; electric utilities are heavily invested in coal companies and in uranium interests; and so on.

The banks and financial institutions have invested heavily in new construction loans to the utilities and the energy companies. Their interests are closely linked to the security and growth of these industries.

5. Utility Law

The basic principle of law for utility regulatory agencies in the various states is to guarantee to the IOUs a dollar percentage return, based on the electric rates, sufficient to attract new investment capital. This means that the public utility commission's members must promulgate electric rate schedules which assure these privately-owned utility monopolies a rate of return which keeps their stocks and bonds attractive to purchasers in the stock and bond markets. The electric energy economy is arranged so that the utility companies practically cannot fail. Moreover, all of the political/financial dynamics of their "arrangement" are intended to encourage more growth, of the same type, which they presently manage to control.

But this industry is now faced by some of the most awesome challenges it has ever faced. There are chinks in the armor of this behemoth system which make it vulnerable to some very important new demands for sharing decision-making prerogatives with citizens. Many segments of the nation are newly aware that traditional utility decision-makers have a set of interests which run counter to the best interests of the public. Citizens now rank environmental safeguards and energy conservation at a very high level of priority in making public policy decisions, a new phenomenon in energy circles.

II. Energy Issues—Or, Handles for Organizing

Issues which now represent points of entry for public input, for shaping energy policy, include the following:

A. Nuclear Hazards

Nuclear power has been rapidly expanding before sufficient knowledge and capacity have been acquired to dispose of the vast quantities of long-lasting and highly hazardous nuclear wastes which are generated. Moreover, the industry has not been sufficiently candid with the public about the risks and hazards of each of the various stages of the nuclear fuel cycle. The potential of vast health hazards to the public in the *normal* operation of the nuclear fuel cycle is only beginning to be understood by the public at large. The cavalier disregard for public well-being in the rapid expansion of nuclear energy has newly awakened large segments of the public to the hazards of placing such vast authority over energy decision in the hands of a relatively small clique of closely closeted energy czars whose primary interests are profit.

B. Increasing Costs of Energy

The public is only beginning to experience rapid increases in energy costs. These increases are just starting because the impact of vast new nuclear and coal construction programs and far more difficult conventional fuel processing requirements is only beginning to be reflected in utility bills. It has been assumed that the American public will pay any amount necessary to be able to increase its energy consumption. It has been assumed that everyone agrees that the level of energy consumed is directly proportional to the quality of life, and that the public will insist upon higher and higher energy consumption.

These views are now being vigorously challenged. The public, more-over, is beginning to understand that a rigidly mechanistic and depersonalized style of life, derived from a high-technology way of life, is being forced upon us by ethical considerations that are solely monetary at their root level of value judgment. The public is begin-ning to say: Who are you to decide for us?! The cost of energy must be commensurate with our maintenance of human dignity and the survival of a liveable planet.

C. Employment/Unemployment

Mechanization and automation of industrial processes has been possible as growth of energy supply replaced man (people) power. In the past, the cost of energy has been lower than the cost of labor; therefore labor has been casually displaced in our industrial and cybernated economy. Therefore, machinery has displaced muscle as the lever for progress. In these last few decades of cheap energy and high industrial capacity at low energy cost, new employment require-ments have almost been enough to keep all Americans at work (only 6 percent unemployment, which many think is far too high!). But as more and more machines have displaced labor, it has required increasingly larger amounts of energy to displace each worker. The machines became more and more costly. We have now reached a point of diminishing returns in the equation of BTU-per-job cost equals labor cost. Moreover, the high cost in human dignity of widespread unemployment and installation of work minding machines is cause for social reevaluation of job displacing energy use.

Now, the general public is beginning to think that use of free solar energy resources for space and water heating can soon reduce the capital outlay for new centralized energy resources. Moreover, solar energy installations can be owned by homeowners and small business people, and not necessarily by utility companies. Though capitalizing this enterprise is a major block to the installation of solar energy, the public understands the large benefits to be derived to them if they can own some of their own energy resources.

The traditional engineering firms and the utilities, however, fear the displacement of their traditional dominance of this market. Water and space heating equipment in homes and businesses can substan-tially reduce the demand for new, high-cost, central generating plants and can, in the process, decentralize job creation. This can spread new employment demand widely over existing trades and industries. For example, the installation of flat plate collectors for home hot water systems would employ carpenters, sheet metal workers, glaziers, electricians, plumbers, roofers and laborers in every village, town and city in the country. The employment potentials of solar strategies for energy are vastly greater than are the job-creating potentials for any central generating plants. Moreover, the cost effectiveness of solar space heating equipment increases where the demand (need) for space heating is greatest.

D. Decentralizing Decision Making

With the power to control goes the power to profit. The energy companies have worked assiduously to persuade the public that you and I can't beat the system, and that control of energy costs is impossible. If it were possible, they claim, they would reduce the cost of energy provided to us. Citizen strategies to change energy priorities must include the goal of decentralizing the control of energy resources. Ivan Illich and Amory Lovins have written persuasively on this issue.[3] When hydro-electric dams were built on a small scale, they were controlled by local authorities. Mammoth dams are controlled by central governments or huge corporations. Small-scale thermal plants can be owned and controlled by communities; but large thermal plants can be financed and operated only by the largest corporations or units of government. To maximize citizen control of energy policies, future energy construction should look to units of energy generation which are owned and controlled as close to the point of use as possible. These types of energy generation may cost more per kilowatt hour of generation than the *older* centralized plants; they will probably be no more expensive than *new* coal or nuclear plants. Some types of small-scale electric generation have been heavily polluting and this must be avoided. But the solar-related scenarios for new generating potential are largely nonpolluting, and they have very large generating potential—though they are most efficient when used in tandem with traditional thermal or hydro plants. The major political/economic block to going solar is the disincentive this may represent to the existing energy companies. Since those who hold energy power today are opposed to energy choices which lead to decentralized control, how can the public intervene to wrest control of energy choices from the current czars of energy decision making?

Let us be clear that the foes of decentralized energy control are the secretary of energy, the U.S. Department of Energy, the best-known oil companies, the uranium companies, General Electric, Westinghouse, the largest natural gas companies, and some of the labor union leadership which is closely related to the superenergy conglomerates.

Identifying Organizable Issues Related to Energy

The big, general issue underlying every other one is the rate of population or industrial growth which is anticipated or planned for by your state and locality. Each of the following issues is related to the rate of growth issues. You and your group will ultimately have to reach a decision about your philosophy on desirable levels of growth in order to have anything like a consistent philosophy related to any of the rest of the items listed below. The philosophy of this writer is that humankind, and each of us, will be better off if we can decide to try to attain as close to a steady state economy as we can achieve. This goal needs to be pursued while at the same time equitably spreading the benefits of our economy to every citizen. There can be no left-outs in any just community or state.

A. Siting New Plants

Utility plans to site new multimegawatt thermal generating plants in your region, or near your town, represent an effort to assure rapid population and economic growth in your region, or to export your resource base for the benefit of distant population groups. Most of these plants will take billions of dollars to build which might, alternatively, be used for other types of economic enterprise more suited to your community and the needs of its current population. It will require vast quantities of capital investment for a supporting infrastructure (mining, processing, transportation and waste disposal); it is apt to offer a relatively low net energy return (i.e., the energy investment to generate the electricity will almost equal the energy output); it may represent an effort to make your town an energy exporter for the benefit of a distant group, polluting your environment for the benefit of others; it will not create many new job opportunities to run the plant; it may swamp your town with construction personnel with great demand for high-cost services, leaving your community with costly tax burdens when they leave at the end of construction. Moreover, and most ominous to community well-being, is that a new political-economic power structure will be introduced to your community, with resources capable of overwhelming every other influential group and of dominating decision-making for the next several generations.

Do you want it? Do you need it? Did anyone ask you? Where does the authority rest for deciding these questions? Answer: usually in

your state's energy facility siting council or similar agency; or the
state department of energy; or your legislature and/or governor.

Such plants must run a long gamut of administrative and planning
hurdles before any energy is generated. Each step represents a possible
point of blockage. Don't assume there are many opponents to
building and operating such a plant. There are only a few, and most
of these persons or groups have very little money. They do have some
substantial tools to work with, however, in terms of protective
environmental and procedural laws. These same handles for restraint
are available to you and your local organization. Expertise to help
you is often available if you look for it in the right places. (See
bibliography.)

B. Siting New Transmission Facilities

Energy generating plants require massive support networks of
transmission lines, railroad rights-of-way, truck ways, pipelines, load-
ing docks, and waste dumping. Do you think these things are good
neighbors? You will be told that these changes are not hard to live
with. Don't believe it! You will be offered substantial rewards for
giving up your environment. Assess the truth and final costs before
taking your reward (bribe?). Remember, you are accepting payment
for giving up your children's environment, too. And their children's!
And their children's too! Also, there are not many places you can run
to that have not already been turned into energy "slave territory."

Normally, the siting of these dumps and rights-of-way requires
that the energy companies file environmental impact statements with
respective government agencies. The agencies are programmed to
favor development—so don't assume they will be very critical of the
EIS. Challenge the EIS, if it does not truly describe the full cost of
environmental degradation that will take place if such developments
occur. Who will pay what prices? Who will gain what benefits? Are
the costs worth the risks and degradation? Who are the chief
beneficiaries and who the chief losers? Who is serving as trustee and
protector for the public interest? Are these conservators functioning
effectively?

C. Sewer Plant Expansion

Effective control of waterway pollution is absolutely essential for
good public health. Treatment of human sewage is a very important
part of water treatment to prevent pollution. But modern sewage
treatment is archaic in relation to good ecological planning. Our

contemporary sewage systems are energy inefficient and represent an accommodation to a planetary occupancy code which is untenable.

The use of septic systems is also untenable in any heavily populated region. Concerned citizens can stop the wild population growth rates by refusing to enlarge the traditional sewage systems. We must move quickly to systems of sewage composting which bring people into a responsible ecological cycle of living gently with nature, rather than trying to force nature into an unforgiving pattern of continuous degradation.

D. Suburban Development—Land Use Planning

New housing developments are gobbling up prime agricultural land at a rapid rate. Sewer connections for new housing make necessary vast new expenditures for water pollution control and new energy resources. Providing the wide range of schooling, police, fire, and health services needed by a new population is a high-cost enterprise. It is the citizens of long-time residency in any area on whom the largest costs for new housing developments will fall. Costs for new developments should be forced upon the developers and the new residents. Such developments have extra high energy costs. Accommodating population growth in the older areas of towns and cities is very much more energy efficient, and ultimately gives to long-time residents many of the financial benefits of new population development, rather than transferring these benefits to outsiders.

Adoption of strict statewide land-use planning requirements which are obligatory for county planning is essential to maintain high environmental standards in a region. Citizen organizations can use these guidelines and procedures to help them organize for good and effective community life. There are wide ramifications for energy planning in a good land-use law. See to it; demand its enforcement.

E. Energy Use Forecasts

The IOUs have every incentive to overforecast the demand for future energy. There is currently a 30 to 35 percent overcapacity to meet current national energy demand. Current consumers are paying dearly for this overcapacity. It is in anticipation of rapid population growth and rapid growth of consumer energy demand that the utilities have already overbuilt large central generating plants. But, in point of fact, the growth in energy demand has been declining in most regions of the country for the past several years. There are probably a variety of reasons for this; one of them is surely the

increasing costs of energy. We in the United States have many
options to reduce our rate of demand of energy, since we have
traditionally been so insensitive and careless in our end use of energy.
Conservation efforts have already succeeded in reducing our demand
without lowering our standards of living. Many experts think that we
could further reduce our use of energy by as much as 50 percent
without lowering our standard of living. Rather, they argue, our life
style, standards could rise, because we could use our saved money
more productively on other, far more important things. These savings
would be achieved by reducing both utility service costs and the huge
capital costs of new generators.

If these kinds of energy savings could be achieved, the energy not
wasted would be energy gained at little capital cost for allocation to
new energy demand. The conservationist attempts to find new energy
sources have caused official state and national agencies to substan-
tially reduce their energy forecasts of demand during the next two or
three decades. The IOUs and some of the publicly owned utilities
have, nonetheless, been very reluctant to reduce their own energy
forecasts. This would reduce their corporate growth and earnings
potentials. It would tend to put a lid on the corporate careers of their
executives.

But the contradictions between corporate and state (and regional)
energy forecasts represent a handle for organizational strategy; they
also represent a handle for organizations to help their members save
both money and the environment in which they live.

F. Total Energy Generation

The potential of towns and cities, or rural areas, to meet part of
their energy needs from local power sources or from ambient environmental conditions, can serve as a high potential incentive for some
community members to participate actively in citizen groups focused
upon energy issues. Certainly installation of solar water heating
systems—perhaps on a cluster-housing basis—is a good way to start.
Or there may be manufacturing plants in the area with high potential
for installation of cogenerative power equipment. In some states the
Public Utility Commission has required a local utility to purchase
locally generated power for distribution to its customers through
existing service connections. Wind generators may meet a significant
part of an energy load in a particular region, and efforts can be made
to have this energy plugged into existing utility lines. The meters
which measure consumer use can be matched with meters which
measure energy contributions to the system.

The U.S. Department of Energy Newsletter[4] has predicted that by 1986 panels of photovoltaic cells can be meeting household energy needs on a cost basis competitive with new coal or nuclear generating plants. That is high-cost energy by today's standards of experience, but it has the major advantage of freeing consumers from dependence (at least to some degree) on the utility companies. For citizen organizations the potential of helping people to work toward energy independence is a very heady brew. Mixing this potential with assistance to citizens in organizing community greenhouses, community organic gardening enterprises, waste composting, cooperative natural food outlets, and cooperative weatherizing and energy conservation strategies in the community can lead to significantly changed and improved life styles for all the people in the community.

G. Increasing Utility Rates

There is no place in the country where energy costs are not increasing. They will continue to rise steeply as repayment schedules for new plants begin to be applied to future rates of energy use. The various public utility commissions really have little control over these rising rates. All they can do is try to prevent the utilities from charging more than a reasonable market-share return on their invested capital. Preventing new unneeded capital investment is the major control that needs to be exercised, and not many of the commissions are able to do this.

But rising utility costs are obviously a concern of consumers. And citizen organizations ought to vent their rage over these costs. Translating rage into effective handles for action for energy change is the challenge organizations face. If the organization leaders have any sophistication, they will recognize that membership education about the true causes of rising energy costs is essential. Increase in demand is the major culprit. Conservation of energy is the first line of defense. And decentralizing control over energy decisions is the first priority strategy. Organizing handles to achieve these objectives are:

1. Buy out the IOU and create a *municipal* utility district, if you live in a city. If you live in the country, form a *public* utility district (or people's utility district) or electric cooperative to meet your energy needs. Return energy decisions to a level of political debate and decision-making close to the citizens. Educate the citizenry to local self-sufficiency as much as possible.

2. Some public utility commissions allow the utilities to include in their rate base a "construction work in progress" component. Theo-

retically, only in publicly owned utilities (where rate payers are the share holders) do the rate payers pay for current construction costs. The rate payers of IOUs do not pay for such costs because they don't assume the risks of unsuccessful building projects. These risks are borne by the shareholders and bondholders, who later collect a benefit in the form of profit for risk undertaken—why else have an investor-owned utility? But some PUCs have allowed CWIP (construction work in progress) costs to be included in IOU rate bases. This fosters generation and transmission construction and growth. It does this at risk and cost to current rate payers who may possibly never receive a benefit. CWIP should be abolished.

3. Utility advertising was included in the rate base charged consumers on the assumption that increased scale of demand could reduce per kilowatt cost. Today that assumption is no longer true. Increased demand increases the cost of the kilowatts consumed by everyone. It is not in the interest of the individual consumer, or the public at large, to increase demand. Therefore, it is not appropriate for the public utility commissions to allow the utility to charge consumers for advertising which is primarily of benefit to stock and bond holders. This is an issue to organize around.

4. Is the availability of utility services optional to life in modern towns and cities? Can one survive without water, electricity, or natural gas if this is the primary heating fuel? Should public policy allow the utility to cut off service to customers if for some reason there is nonpayment? Justice requires a "no" answer.

Should utilities be allowed to charge more for the first 500 or 1,000 kilowatts or 10 or 20 therms of natural gas than for the following 1,000 kilowatts or 30 therms? Traditionally, and in most cases today, rate bases for utilities have been allowed to be smaller for energy in large amounts than in small amounts. The small users pay proportionally more for energy than the big users who, in toto, account for the largest amount of energy use. Obviously, this discriminates against conservation of energy. These companies also assume that having the use of any form of energy is a privilege, and not a right.

There are proposals to change this approach. They often go by the name of life-line rates. Under the life-line approach, every consumer is assumed to have a need for a minimum amount of energy, which should be priced at the smallest charge per kilowatt hour. The consumer under life-line rates is guaranteed a minimum of energy at the lowest price. If the household uses more than the minimum "conservation" block of energy, it then pays a higher rate for the next block. The commercial and industrial users under life-line rates do not then receive a subsidy from household users for their rate of charge.

Most consumer organizations advocate life-line rates as a matter of justice to poor people and as a justifiable rate for middle-income householders. This is another organizable issue.

5. Time-of-day pricing is an approach to the cost of energy which recognizes that, for most utilities, energy delivered at the times of day which are peak-use hours costs most for the utility to deliver. If householders, or industries, would time their demand to avoid peak-use hours, they could, given the assumption of peak-rate-designed utility rates, receive a lower rate. Or utilities could install automatic shut-off and turn-on switches to appliances (like freezers and hot-water heaters, washers and dryers), which would schedule their use to make them conserve energy by limiting their operation to off-peak hours. This would limit the need of utilities to build high-cost generating plants to be available on a standby basis for only short periods of time during the year.

Consumer-related organizations should work to require time-of-day pricing as a part of normal rate bases. An organizing issue.

6. When costs of oil and coal rapidly escalated after the 1973 oil embargo, utilities across the country were given automatic adjustments in their rates, so that they could pass on to consumers costs which, in some instances, they could not have foreseen in planning rate base requests. Since then, however, there have been many proven instances where fuel cost increases were inappropriately included in the rate base. Where utilities own all or part of the company providing the fuel supply to generating plants, there has been special reason for concern.

Some public utilities commissions are reviewing the appropriateness of automatic fuel adjustment clauses. This is a matter which deserves scrutiny and appropriate action by citizen organizations.

7. "Phantom taxes" is the term Environmental Action has used to publicize the remarkable phenomenon by which utilities charge customers for taxes which are levied on utility services by the government, collected by the utility and left unpaid by the utility to the IRS, thereby enriching its own coffers. This practice is widely followed and is, in many instances, not illegal. It occurs, at least in part, because of the fast tax write-off for capital investment which IRS now allows utilities.

The disparity between the taxes collected by the utility for payment, and the actual payments made, however, can be quite shocking. The highly complex system of cost and profit accounting used by utilities has led many an observer to conclude that nothing short of public acquisition of private (monopoly service) utilities can adequately protect the public interest from exploitation. By all means, determine and publicize the amount of phantom taxes your local utilities collect and do not pay.

8. The utilities' representatives who appear before public utility commissions to secure increased rate structures and benefits are usually very competent, well-prepared, highly paid, and adept. The representatives of citizen groups are usually volunteers who don't even have secretarial services, not to speak of legal counsel, extensive research facilities, or wide access to political influence. They usually are competent, but sometimes they are not as articulate or armed with comprehensive data, and often their perspectives and presentations are marred by inadequate research and legal experience. Should the interest of the public, generally, be less well represented than the interests of share and bond holders before an official rate-setting body of state government? Citizen organizations are demanding that a qualified, legally trained and experienced person serve as an intervenor and representative (an *ombudsman*) in behalf of rate payers as a counterpart to the representatives of the utilities.

The ways in which this can be accomplished vary. It would be possible by having: a state-paid utility ombudsman connected with the state department of energy; an independent expert whose pay is derived from a small charge added to each consumer's utility bill; or a consumer affairs unit of state government could hire staff who are charged to represent the public interest before rate-setting bodies. Citizen organizations might make this a key demand, as it relates to fairness in setting utility rates.

9. Many utilities require consumers to make a deposit of money to them before service hook-up is provided. Or they might have hook-up requirements which a particular household may or may not be able to meet. Where such conditions of nonservice exist, and if consumers are often denied service as a result of them—or especially if there is discrimination between types of consumers in administering the conditions—a citizens' organization should quickly become informed about these circumstances and take action to eliminate discrimination and/or nonservice.

The National Energy Act, finally passed by the U.S. Congress in 1978, mandates to utilities that they *consider* adopting rate schedules which incorporate these concepts: cost of service, declining block rates, time-of-day rates, interruptible rates, and various load management techniques. Public hearings must be held prior to the utility's making decisions on these matters. Citizens should use these hearings as occasions to be heard.

Types of Organizations Working to Achieve Energy Change

A. Special Interest Organizations

A special interest organization, by its nature, is focused upon either a particular objective to be achieved, or it mobilizes a special constituency to work in behalf of its particular interests. There are many types of special interest organizations related to energy issues on the state level. For instance, citizen groups to oppose nuclear power; efforts to organize a people's utility district; a campaign to reduce utility costs; or to lower noise pollution of a power plant; or to oppose a transmission line; or to reduce generating plant smoke emission, and so on. All of them have merit in terms of achieving some energy policy change. But it is often only when such groups coalesce in particular campaigns for change that they attain their greatest potential for influencing public policy.

A typical statewide coalition for citizen participation in the control of nuclear power was Oregonians for Nuclear Safeguards. At the time it was organized, in 1974, there were several active groups in the state which were so opposed to *any* nuclear plants under any conditions at all that they would not participate in this coalition. Standing behind Oregonians for Nuclear Safeguards were the following: The Ecumenical Ministries of Oregon; The Center for Environmental Action; Oregon Environmental Council; Oregon League of Women Voters; Tri-County Committee for New Politics; Oregon Democratic Platform Committee, and many county Democratic committees; the Retail Clerks Union; the Longshoremen's Union; the Audubon Society; the Sierra Club; the Friends of the Earth; Oregon Student Public Interest Group; Women's International League for Peace and Freedom; citizen groups in Linn, Benton, Polk, Douglas, Jackson, Josephine, Klamath Falls, Deschutes, Clatsop, and Coos counties; the Eugene Future Power Committee (which was one of the best informed of the local groups); the Senior Citizens Council; and the Grey Panthers; also student organizations, and especially student environmental groups on university campuses.

In every state there will be similar types of groups which have a high potential for participation in energy action coalitions. Common Cause is often focused upon energy-related issues and their membership can be counted on as allies if they are currently working on a correlative issue. Organic gardening clubs, natural food cooperatives, solar energy organizations, ecology centers, National Health Federation chapters, alternative energy groups, appropriate technology groups, all represent types of groups whose members are apt to be very interested in citizen energy organizing.

Besides these types of citizen groups, there are a wide range of specialized research organizations that offer citizen groups assistance in the form of literature, legal counsel, expert testimony, research aid, and sometimes funding. Identify these groups in your state by contacting your state environmental council or the antinuclear organizations in your state.

Groups in the headlines in 1978 included the Clamshell Alliance, Crabshell Alliance, Abalone Alliance, and similar groups, which are taking direct action to close down nuclear generating plants. The tens of thousands of people who have signed the antinuclear petitions of the Task Force Against Nuclear Pollution, Inc., have communicated effectively to their representatives and senators in Washington. Such efforts are good means of citizen impact on energy policy.[5]

During sessions of any state legislatures, there is apt to be a cluster of citizen groups working for legislation to encourage energy conservation, or for the "soft" energy alternatives to nuclear and coal multimegawatt plants. Assistance to these coalitions can be very important in swaying legislators who are already under the influence of big power interests.

B. Mass-Based Organizations

The churches have had special interest over the years in supporting citizen organizations which are widely representative of every group in subcommunities of large cities. In the past, these organizations have been a voice for people normally unheard in the political life of a large metropolis. The organization galvanizes the interests of these citizens and assures effective participation of them in the give-and-take of power and benefit trade-offs. Organizations in Chicago are particularly well-known: The Woodlawn Organization; Organization of the Southwest Communities; Northwest Community Organization; Austin Community Organization, among others.

A widely based citizen group which has particularly tackled issues of environmental pollution and utility rate issues has been the Citizens

Against Pollution, which became the Community Action Program in Illinois. CAP (Citizens Action Project) organizations have been created in a number of other states in recent years, California being one of the most active.

Massachusetts Fair Share is an approach to mass-based citizen organizing, which is being replicated in various states. Oregon Fair Share is one of the most recent organizational efforts undertaken. The Fair Share organizations attempt to help their members identify local and state-wide issues which lend themselves to citizen action issue resolution, and energy and utility rate issues are high on their agenda for action.

ACORN (Arkansas Community Organization for Reform Now) is an approach to mass-based citizen organization which has won wide acclaim for success in helping people achieve real victories in energy-related matters. Their organizing energies are now at work in numerous communities across the country. To create new mass-based citizen organizations requires careful planning and adequate financial resources, but this is a course well worth pursuing.

C. Party Politics

Many concerned citizens have taken the time and energy to become active in regular Democratic and Republican partisan politics as a way of impacting energy policy. The popularity of Governor Jerry Brown's antinuclear politics in California, and the popularity of his encouragement of solar energy tax incentives has not been lost on other politicians. President Jimmy Carter's energy conservation leanings won him many an environmentalist's support in 1976. But his wavering encouragement of the solar options, and his apparent support for nuclear fission energy options have left his ardent environmentalist supporters confused. National and state party platforms are becoming anti-nuclear power and pro-energy conservation. State politicians will in part be influenced by understanding where precinct workers stand on these issues.

Some minority electoral party organizations focus on energy policies. The New America Movement is a socialist-oriented political movement trying to attract middle-Americans. Its energy perspective is apparently anti-nuclear energy, and it is concerned about utility rates.

The U.S. Labor Party is a political party of the far right which seeks to expand nuclear power proliferation at home and abroad. It favors the rapid development of the nuclear fast breeder reactor and rapid research and development of nuclear fusion power.

Conclusion

Current energy policy in the United States is being shaped by the forces of congressional debate, federal budget allocations, defense policy, corporation energy development plans, and state energy policies. Citizens are also involved in three ways as people who have: a) hope for the future; b) habits of energy use; c) organizations to register their energy policy concerns. These three modes of involvement are interrelated. Our social hopes—the kind of society we envision—animate our politics and our personal energy use. But to put legs under our expectations, we need concrete action handles and organizational methods.

The nation's energy problems and choices impel citizens to enter the energy policy debate with a clearer understanding of a desirable future, a practical present, and the political ways to get from here to there. If the churches view energy choices as a context for value reflection and crucial ethical choice, then the churches must foster organized citizen participation in energy politics concerned with conservation, appropriate, limited energy production, and fairer distribution of energy resources.

The questions that need discussion by citizen groups, including the churches, preparatory to participation in policy formulation, are the following:

1. How should citizens participate in energy policy formulation?

2. What are the long-range implications of what seem initially to be only immediate energy questions?

3. How much "development" can be sustained by our region without straining the eco-system?

4. How much energy can typical families consume without damaging the environment? Take into account the amount of energy required by major employers in your region. Take into account the way most energy in your region is generated.

5. Are the soft energy paths superior to the hard paths? In what respect?

6. What implications for the next generations are there in the energy choices before us?

7. Who should be making decisions about the above questions? How do we go about influencing the people who are closest to such decision-making? Who will do it?

Chapter 6:

Exodus from Nuclear Bondage*

by Mark Reader†

Nuclear power creates the unattainable and undesirable need for permanent and total control of people and of nature as a means of avoiding nuclear catastrophe, while it generates those counterforces which prevent its realization.

Present-day energy choices are driving the world to the brink of thermonuclear war and environmental exhaustion. As nation-states seek energy independence, they are committing themselves to the nuclear alternative and, with that, assuring atomic weapons proliferation and risking the radioactive contamination of the biosphere through the manufacture of extremely long-lasting, carcinogenic wastes which the human species does not know how to dispose of.

What is most at issue in the energy debate is the Nuclear Age itself. The energy situation is forcing us to decide whether humanity can learn to live with the atom, or whether we must renounce its use in human affairs.

---

*Portions of this article were adapted from an essay that appeared in *Peace and Change*, v. 1 (spring 1978), and from remarks delivered at Ghost Ranch, Abiquiu, New Mexico, July 1978.

†Associate Professor of Political Science, Arizona State University, Tempe, Arizona.

Advocates of fission power challenge these reflections. They believe that the nuclear commitment can, and must, be extended without delay to keep civilization afloat and misery at a distance. They contend that we can have our energy cake and eat it too. Nuclear and solar together. What's more, they say, there is little chance of halting the process of A-bomb and radioactive waste proliferation. Japan and some European nations are determined to reprocess plutonium in order to get free of American, Soviet and Arab energy dominance; and Third World countries will develop a nuclear capacity if only to gain economic and political parity on the world stage.

The antinuclear movement focuses on the certainty that nuclear power will take a heavy toll of human life and liberty. The pronuclear enthusiasts point to the possibility that homo sapiens could end up dead if it tried to do *without* it. But the reality is that we can't live *with* nuclear power's physical and social fallout.

Social Consequences of Nuclear Power

As both commitment and resistance to atomic power as a way of solving the world's energy crisis grow, it is becoming increasingly evident that fission power—in both its military and energy applications—now constitutes an assault on human freedom.

This idea of the fundamental incompatibility between nuclear energy and democracy is relatively new and, consequently, not very well understood. Indeed, the idea is so at odds with conventional wisdom that most official and popular discussions of the energy crisis, and the atom's place in it, go on without it. Energy decisions are thought of as primarily economic and technological, with publics expected to play supporting roles to elites who set energy policy. Because energy questions are rarely put to the vote, many people pliantly accept the claim that all they need do to assure themselves a limitless supply of energy is maintain "eternal vigilance" over the nuclear fuel cycle.[1] That idea seems more readily apparent, at any rate, than one which proposes that there might be some connection between energy choices and personal liberties.[2]

Indeed, the technological skewing of modern culture is so complete that it affects every side of the nuclear debate. Thus, as recently as 1976, when the nuclear energy question was put to the voters in six western American states, it was conceived of as a problem of "safety," with antinuclear forces calling for a nuclear reactor moratorium on safety and financial grounds and nuclear proponents complaining that such a pause would arbitrarily punish an industry whose safety and employment records were second to none. Those few voices that tried to deal with atomic energy from a political and ethical perspective were drowned out in the acrimonious exchange of statistics and ill will which passed as debate.

In retrospect, however, the safe energy campaign probably marked the last time in America when the nuclear debate would, and could, be cast almost exclusively in economic and technological terms. Even then, a series of seemingly disconnected events was forcing the presidential candidates to consider the political implications of the nuclear alternative[3] and, within six months of the elections, the Clamshell Alliance had succeeded in dramatizing its view that atomic reactors posed a de facto threat to human life, liberty and happiness.[4]

Atomic reactors for electricity generation are only the most visible of six stages in the nuclear fuel cycle. (See chart 6.) This cycle involves uranium mining and milling, enrichment into usable fuel, fabrication into fuel rods, use in electricity-generating stations, the option of reprocessing spent fuel, and storage of high-level radioactive wastes, as well as burial of low-level radioactive tools, equipment, clothing, and fluids. Transportation occurs throughout the nuclear fuel cycle, with accidents and theft real occurrences—a truck full of wastes turns over on a highway with people driving by, a shipment of uranium never reaches its destination.

Management of existing nuclear wastes will cost taxpayers tens of billions of dollars, without real assurance that proposed methods of waste storage will be safe for the hundreds of millennia that they remain radioactive. One of the major waste products of the nuclear fuel cycle is the nuclear reactor itself. After thirty to forty years of use, the electricity-generating station deteriorates to the point that it must be "decommissioned," at additional cost and with the need for permanent security. No one actually knows how much this will cost, since the first major decommissionings have not yet taken place.

The nuclear fuel cycle requires continuous, though not always effective, surveillance. The cycle needs people watching the machines, machines watching machines, and machines and people watching people, to protect against nonroutine releases of, or exposure to, radiation. As atomic power proliferates, nuclear fuel cycles overlap, and whole cultures must be organized to guard against nuclear hazards. The outcome is antidemocratic social control.

Threat to Civil Liberties

As presently conceived, the theory of the basic incompatibility between atomic power and civil liberties runs something like this:

In order to avoid nuclear contingency—accident, theft of fission-able materials, sabotage of facilities, war, blackmail, uncontrolled protests, or clandestine atomic bomb making—people who are enthralled to the atom must exert enormous amounts of social control over the whole of an everexpanding nuclear fuel cycle for extended periods of time and even then be prepared to experience nuclear breakdowns.

According to this view, what the National Council of Churches said about the potential totalitarian characteristics of the plutonium economy of tomorrow may be applied with equal truth to the actual workings of the fission economy of today: "the drastic nature of the nuclear threat is apt to elicit a drastic police response. Even these measures, however repressive, might in the end prove ineffective."[5]

First, it is noted, the nuclear option intensifies the very conflicts it must avoid if the nuclear fuel cycle is to be secured. It does so by aggravating political, economic and ego inequalities—either by dividing the human community into nuclear *have* and nuclear *have-not* nations and persons, as has happened in world politics from 1945 onward; or by making some nuclear *haves* more equal than others by denying the least-favored equal access to nuclear information and technologies. (It is this latter circumstance which sets up the need for a permanent political intelligence network and information control.)

The result is familiar enough. As the least-favored struggle to free themselves from superpower dominance and secure the equivalent of nuclear parity through military, technological and economic assistance from the superpowers, the number and location of human transactions that must be controlled increases exponentially, even as the atom begins to proliferate globally.[6]

The nuclear paradox is thus set in motion. The more the atom proliferates, the greater the need, and the less the ability, to control it. Dennis Hayes describes the dilemma this way: "Arguments against nuclear power are rooted in a simple paradox. Commercial nuclear power is viable under social conditions of absolute stability and predictability. Yet the mere existence of fission materials undermines the security that nuclear technology requires."[7]

And this is precisely what is happening in the real world today. The need for greater and more sophisticated social controls is increasing directly as are the number of sites at which uranium is being mined, the number of radioactive transportation transactions, the number of enrichment facilities, the number of fabrication plants, the number of reactors, the number of radioactive burial grounds, the number of nuclear technicians, the number of supporting industries, and the number of nuclear decisions and concerns. If Amory Lovins's estimate of the hardware needed to run the nuclear industry over the next generation is even partially correct, one can expect the de facto destruction of democratic culture before the year 2000.[8]

Mason Willrich seems to have anticipated some of the major social costs of nuclear reactor proliferation in an article of May 1975. There he pointed out that an expanded reactor program would require protection against theft and acts of terror; public and/or private paramilitary units to safeguard nuclear power plants and the processes they set in motion; security consciousness in government and in industry which, in turn, would necessitate a security establishment; development of appropriate surveillance technologies to guard against theft and sabotage of nuclear materials; and the need to control "malfunctioning humans" and, by implication, the environments in which they operate.[9] Willrich should also have pointed out that as these requirements become more comprehensive and more permanent, democratic political culture, upon which the actual health of all civil liberties ultimately depends, would itself be elbowed aside to make room for all of the surveillance and supporting infrastructure which the atom requires.

As Lovins argues, the nuclear alternative will culminate in permanent systems of dominance and submission. As significantly, however, it will also require citizens to think like soldiers rather than as free and open people.[10]

The second totalitarian feature present in fission power has been identified more recently by Garrett Hardin, among others.[11] Given a nuclear technology which must be operated without major error for generations, given an exponentially growing number of nuclear transactions and control points, and given the fact that imperfect and free human beings are to be found at more and more interstices of a nuclear fuel cycle becoming universalized—how can the impetus toward police state controls and nuclear catastrophe be avoided?

For the most part, these questions remain unresolved. What is certain, however, is that as nuclear reactors proliferate around the globe, people in both the industrialized and nonindustrialized parts of the world will have to find ways of avoiding police states run, directly or indirectly, by nuclear elites on behalf of nuclear interests. If this is not done, then one can expect both the level of antinuclear violence and repression to rise and the chances of a nuclear catastrophe to increase.

Warning Signs

Public consciousness of the social fallout of nuclear power was heightened as the environmental movement matured and began to see the connections between environmental renewal and social justice.

With the appearance of portions of Lewis Mumford's two-volume *The Myth of the Machine*[12] during the decade of the sixties, it became clear to literate audiences that nuclear reactors were much more than accidental sources of energy developed as a twentieth century afterthought. Rather they could be seen as the necessary culmination of an antihuman technological dynamic and a civilization which had foregone all restraints on power—constitutional and otherwise—long ago. Environmental works like Barry Commoner's *The Closing Circle* completed the picture. Commoner reminded those who had forgotten, and taught many who had never learned, that every human decision, including the nuclear one, carries with it social as well as ecological costs, that radiation is a continuing problem, and that humanity had best get clear about the social costs of doing business if it wished to survive. These and similar lessons led to belated and much-needed environmental legislation at the national level and to a not altogether satisfactory international declaration of environmental rights at Stockholm in 1972.[13]

It was not until 1975, however, that a handful of environmentalists began to talk and write about the negative political costs of atomic power and the inverse relationship between it and democracy. By the end of that year they were beginning to forge intellectual links with peace activists in the common understanding that there never had been—and there never could be—any fundamental difference between the antidemocratic fallout from atomic reactors and from atomic bombs. Both, they were beginning to realize, would lead, as they had already led, to the trammeling of fundamental liberties and to rule by narrow-gauged military-technological elites. The civil liberties case against nuclear reactors was being developed in this way:

> . . . if one faces the issue squarely, one quickly comes to understand that the social costs involved in running [nuclear reactors] . . . will require us, minimally, to continue to exert enormous amounts of control over the everyday lives of people in this and the next generation in order to safeguard these plants against contingencies (read: people) and, simultaneously, prevent the lives of anyone's children from unfolding in ways other than those now narrowly being prescribed by this . . . year's crop of nuclear specialists. Now where have we come across this incessant need for security before, and what did it lead to then? . . . It was

just this sort of argument, because it was out of precisely the same sort of ungovernable circumstance, that helped generate the cold war, containment strategies ... and an unwillingness and/or inability on the part of democratic governments ... to protect even their own people and their own democratic institutions from being subverted by "security needs."[14]

At about the same time, peace activist Sidney Lens put the case against the "peaceful" atom in an influential article entitled "The Doomsday Strategy."

Who will guard against theft of plutonium by terrorist gangs or guerillas? The AEC itself, in the Rosenbaum Report of 1974, hinted that nothing less than a police state will suffice. A million people have already been trained in the handling, moving, and operation of nuclear weapons—each one of whom must be checked for security. Millions more will have to be similarly checked as the reprocessing industry expands.[15]

And Lens added:

"The first and one of the most important lines of defense against groups which might attempt to illegally acquire special nuclear materials to make a weapon is timely and *in-depth intelligence*," says the Rosenbaum Report. "Such intelligence may involve electronic and other means of surveillance, but its most important aspect is *infiltration of groups themselves*." (Emphasis added.) This task, says the report, must be undertaken not by the AEC but by the U.S. Government, including the FBI, CIA and NSA.[16]

Shortly before Lens's article appeared, in a report prepared for the Nuclear Regulatory Commission (NRC), the Mitre Corporation had recommended that in-depth information about terrorist and "other threatening groups" should be obtained by NRC from government intelligence agencies, "including any information indicating a potential threat to the industry generally, or to a specific company."[17] Thus, by the close of 1976, recommendations had been made to government to have the surveillance network follow the nuclear industry wherever, and perhaps however, it might decide to operate. The nuclear fuel cycle, along with its security needs, was expanding exponentially.

What the Public Needs to Know

If, and when, Congress begins investigations into the nuclear cycle's impact on civil liberties,[18] questions of two sorts must be

Chart 6
Vulnerable Points of the Nuclear Fuel Cycle

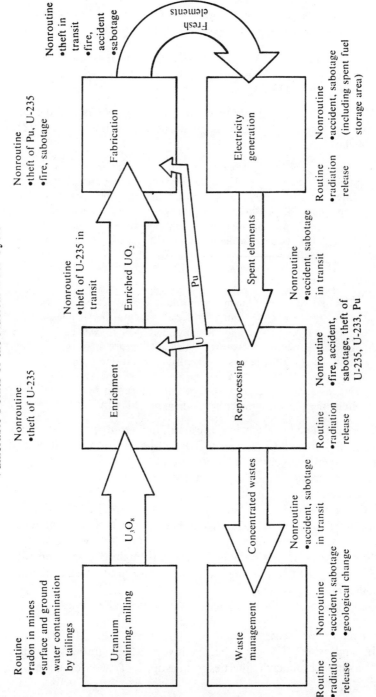

Stages of nuclear fuel cycle where routine radiation releases occur and where nonroutine releases or incidents could occur. Arrows indicate transportation links. U- uranium; UO- uranium dioxide; U_3O_8- uranium oxide; Pu- plutonium. Source: As redrawn from the October 1974—Bulletin of Atomic Scientists.

asked: 1) how many de facto violations of civil liberties have actually taken place in connection with nuclear cycle operation? And as importantly, 2) to what extent is the fission commitment contributing to the erosion of democratic political culture?

In this latter connection, it will be important to get answers to questions such as these:

1. To what extent do local social indicators—like a high crime rate, unemployment, rapid population growth, large-scale illegal immigration, heavy traffic in drugs, a clash of cultures, and a weak tradition of civil liberties—suggest social instability and the need for security precautions at the site of each actual and proposed nuclear reactor, and within the communities in which they operate?

2. To what extent does the safe operation of the nuclear fuel cycle depend upon high levels of information, the quality of education, the availability of widely-shared skills and an enriched and open cultural milieu? Or is a less free life more compatible with the nuclear alternative?

3. To what extent is the nuclear alternative changing the social, economic and political character of the nation by creating new, and potentially antidemocratic industries and habits of thought and action? What are the economic as well as the political costs of these changes?

4. To what extent will it be possible to teach coming generations democratic and nonviolent values, how to live happy and open lives, and how to avoid anxiety in a society geared to the protection of nuclear energy plants whose physical, ethical and human implications have never been fully or publicly explored?

5. To what extent, if any, did Congress—in authorizing the nuclear alternative—inadvertently deny to the states and to the citizens within the states the actual chance of practicing republicanism and of continuing, for very much longer, their lives, their liberties, and their ability to pursue happiness?

How will the nuclear alternative affect our lives and liberties? There are ominous signs of fallout, as both the Three Mile Island reactor accident and the U.S. government's attempt to suppress *The Progressive's* story about the workings of the hydrogen bomb industry now suggest.

Conclusion

The only way out of the deadly nuclear dilemma is to repeal the Nuclear Age. This is the rallying cry around which much of global and domestic energy politics will revolve in the years ahead. At long last—as the control aspects of nuclear power are being felt in higher utility rates, growing fears of nuclear accident-theft-sabotage, more than the random denial of civil liberties, and perpetual rule by elites— people are beginning to tell their governments that they cannot live in freedom or security with nuclear weapons or nuclear reactors at their back doors. Politicians everywhere will simply have to find ways to solve the global energy/political crisis without laying certain disaster on the human species.

More specifically, an emerging coalition of environmental, peace, citizens' and religious groups are beginning to realize that if the governments of the world were really thinking clearly about their commitment to global peace and freedom, they would give up the nuclear illusion and try to settle the world's energy crisis by developing benign energy technologies and by sharing the world's resources.

The only way to break out of nuclear bondage is to declare quits of the nuclear game, wholly. The nuclear fuel cycle is a no-win contest. Within the terms of the game, humanity cannot survive. The way out takes four steps.

1. Our government can declare a moratorium on further construction of all nuclear reactors and announce our intention to phase out nuclear energy sources as soon as technologically and humanly feasible.

2. We must declare an intention to get out of the nuclear weapons business, through staged disarmament. The United States should make a unilateral gesture to begin this process.

3. We must couple the question of nuclear reactors and nuclear weapons with the question of social injustice, including energy injustice, worldwide. We must work out global agreements to meet minimum energy supply needs interdependently, rather than by urging each nation to become energy-independent.

4. We must overcome the fear of not having enough without nuclear power. We can do without nuclear power by combining serious efforts at conservation and efficiency with the development of alternative energy options, which would replace nuclear power as soon as possible.

The risks of abandoning nuclear power are much less troubling than are the risks of continuing to develop a nuclear society. The nuclear route involves the high probability of major destruction; the nonnuclear option entails further experimentation with benign technologies and social forms, which, after all, is consistent with the purpose of life itself.

Chart 7
Nuclear Threats to Human Survival*

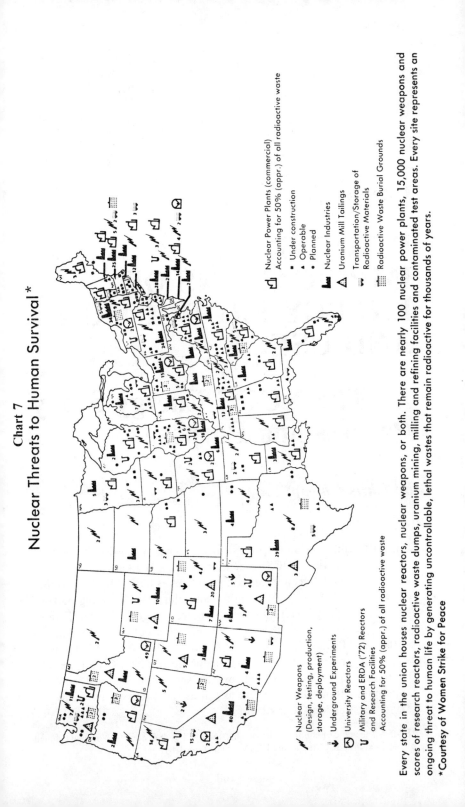

Nuclear Weapons
(Design, testing, production, storage, deployment)

→ Underground Experiments

Ⓧ University Reactors

U Military and ERDA (72) Reactors and Research Facilities
Accounting for 50% (appr.) of all radioactive waste

Nuclear Power Plants (commercial)
Accounting for 50% (appr.) of all radioactive waste
■ Under construction
▲ Operable
● Planned

Nuclear Industries

△ Uranium Mill Tailings

↝ Transportation/Storage of Radioactive Materials

Radioactive Waste Burial Grounds

Every state in the union houses nuclear reactors, nuclear weapons, or both. There are nearly 100 nuclear power plants, 15,000 nuclear weapons and scores of research reactors, radioactive waste dumps, uranium mining, milling and refining facilities and contaminated test areas. Every site represents an ongoing threat to human life by generating uncontrollable, lethal wastes that remain radioactive for thousands of years.

*Courtesy of Women Strike for Peace

Chapter 7:

ETHICAL IMPLICATIONS OF ENERGY PRODUCTION AND USE

A. The NCCC Energy Study Process and Purpose

by Chris Cowap*

In 1974, the National Council of Churches of Christ Division of Church and Society (DCS) executive, Lucius Walker, handed me a folder with one letter in it, asked me to "act as liaison to this group," and assured me that "it won't take much time; they're doing most of the work." "They" were Doctors Margaret Mead and René Dubos, who at the request of DCS were cochairing a committee of inquiry on the use of plutonium as a commercial nuclear fuel. In September 1975, they presented their report, dropping the NCCC and me into the middle of a full-time war which shows no signs of abating. Sometimes I think the issues are as hot as radioactive wastes and will take at least as long to cool off.

*Staff Associate for Economic Justice, Division of Church & Society, National Council of the Churches of Christ in the U.S.A., New York City.

The Chronology of the Council's Involvement

Review of NCCC policy and resolutions reveals almost no engagement with the energy issue until 1975. The Council, with most of society, pigeon-holed energy questions as *technical* or *political*. One early note was sounded in 1960, when general enthusiasm for Eisenhower's "Atoms for Peace" led to the NCCC's "Policy Statement on the Peaceful Uses of Nuclear Energy." While warning about dangers of radioactivity, this statement called for transference of nuclear energy from government control to private enterprise, and for rapid all-out development of nuclear fission as an energy source.

The next decade and a half found the council frequently calling for nuclear disarmament, but silent on *peaceful nuclear technology*. Not until December 1973, responding to the initial shock of OPEC and gasoline shortages, did the council adopt another statement, "The Moral Demands of the Energy Crisis," which called for conservation and reexamination of Christian stewardship in light of energy resource shortages. A pacific prelude, indeed, to the war that broke out in October 1975.

At the October 1975 NCCC Governing Board meeting, the Mead/Dubos Committee of Inquiry proposed a policy statement condemning commercial use of plutonium as a nuclear fuel. During the required six-month reaction period before voting on the statement, the Council (and specifically the Division of Church and Society) found itself embroiled in unprecedented controversy. Many Christian laity (and others) employed in the nuclear industry and electrical utilities vehemently opposed the statement, while strong support was voiced by at least an equal number of concerned citizens. The opposition charged us with gross irresponsibility: the Council had already raised severe questions about coal strip-mining; to ban plutonium, the industry said, was to end nuclear fission; what did we have positively to suggest about energy supplies?

Acknowledging the valid need to explore alternatives, we withdrew the proposed policy statement and substituted the "Resolution on the Plutonium Economy," calling for a moratorium on commercial plutonium use and mandating a broad study on the ethical implications of energy production and use. In March 1976, the resolution was debated extensively (at the time national controversy was raging over the Clinch River plutonium breeder reactor) and overwhelmingly adopted by the NCCC Governing Board.

In the summer of 1976 Katherine Seelman, a political scientist with expertise in science, technology and public policy, was employed as energy resources consultant. I continued with overall administrative responsibility for the project. Preparatory meetings of denominational executives were held. In October, the NCCC Governing Board adopted a resolution calling for stringent international safeguards to prevent the proliferation of nuclear weapons resulting from transfer of "peaceful" nuclear reprocessing technology. The resolution reflected the board's reluctant conclusion that the capacity to generate nuclear energy is inseparable from the capacity to build nuclear weapons.

The Energy Study Panel

In December 1976, the DCS chairperson, Dr. Kenneth Kuntz (Christian Church/Disciples of Christ), appointed the Rev. Joel Thompson (Church of the Brethren) to chair a 120-member Energy Study Panel (ESP). The panel represented expertise in a unique combination of disciplines: theology, ethics, labor, energy industries, technical sciences, social sciences, economics, the environment and consumers. At the core of the panel and acting as its steering committee was the Committee on Energy Policy, representing denominations. This committee had final responsibility for drafting the proposed policy statement.

The study process during 1977 concentrated on identifying the ethical concerns panel members found arising in their various fields; the panel responded to a detailed questionnaire, and the results were formulated and clarified by the theologian/ethicist sector of the panel. (Nothing like this questionnaire had been attempted before; the results are being utilized in President Carter's review of solar energy policy.) Numerous issue papers, representing various points of view, were circulated on specific energy technologies; other study papers dealt with issues such as the health and safety of workers, employment, the disadvantaged and energy rates and services, and other such subjects. A number of panelists also participated in on-site visits to deep and surface coal mines, oil and uranium sites, generating plants, and so on. (These visits were arranged with the cooperation of energy industry representatives on the ESP.) Staff and some panelists also met with executive office staff of the White House.

The panel was drawn together at the Energy Ethics Consultation, October 12-14, 1977, at Stony Point, New York. Present were eighty-two panel members and thirteen observers. Opening speeches by Joel Thompson, William P. Thompson (NCCC president) and Stephen Schneider (a climatologist) set the unique tone of the NCCC's approach to the energy issue: namely, that *energy is a means to achieve social ends,* not an end in itself; therefore the technologies must be in harmony with the social ends desired.

The panel first considered the major categories of social impacts: public policy, social institutions, international relations, environment, food, health/safety, and employment. Each group developed ethical criteria by which an energy policy or technology could be judged. (For instance, health/safety said, "Energy decisions should not place one group at risk for the benefit of an entirely different group.")

The second day was spent in reconstituted small groups, this time technology assessment groups or TAGs on oil and gas, synfuels, coal, conservation, solar/appropriate technology, electricity and two nuclear groups. The task was to assess the assigned technology against ethical criteria. For instance, a nuclear TAG discussed whether nuclear technology was helpful, neutral, or harmful to the health/safety group's criterion. A great deal of technical information was shared in this process, while still keeping the focus on the ethical questions. This was undoubtedly the most frustrating and difficult part of the consultation, perhaps primarily because it demanded a reversal of our usual thinking: instead of taking the *technology* as the given and seeing how the ethical criteria fit in with it, we took the *ethical criteria* as the given and looked at how the technology affected them.

Finally panelists were asked to suggest an energy policy which would not violate the ethical criteria, using the technology assessments. In the event a criterion would be violated by the proposed policy, they were to say why that was acceptable (e.g., identify the tradeoffs). Each group produced a report which was shared in the final plenary. The majority consensus favored a rapid shift away from fossil fuels and nuclear fission toward solar/appropriate technology, with heavy emphasis on the need for conservation. Employment questions were raised, along with the need to ensure equity for the disadvantaged and to ensure that technologies are not so complex and large-scale as to threaten democratic control and participatory decision-making.

Following the groups' reports, a number of other statements were made. These ranged from a powerful report from the Third World Caucus (who correctly termed it "a *majority* minority report") to statements by individuals who, in turn, defended the use of nuclear fission, called for an immediate nuclear shutdown, complained of inadequate industry representation, stressed the necessity of urgent concern for employment, and asked for another conference.

Outcome of the Study

The consultation reports and other papers and experiences from the entire study process were considered by the Committee on Energy Policy as it drafted the proposed policy statement. This was presented for first reading to the May 1978 NCCC Governing Board. Besides board reaction, voluminous other comments were registered throughout the summer with DCS (the final pile measures three feet of paper, a prodigious use of one alternate energy source). Staff and CEP members also met with formal and informal groups of church people to discuss the paper (at Ghost Ranch, Los Alamos, and elsewhere).

The paper was revised after consideration of these reactions, and submitted to the November 1978 NCCC Governing Board meeting, for debate and final vote. By then, however, opposition had solidified. The nuclear industry and utilities openly and effectively solicited their church-affiliated members to register disapproval of the statement. In contrast, the coal sector, which was also stringently challenged in the paper, did not react, while portions of the solar industry, labor, environmentalists, conservationists and minority groups registered strong but less well-orchestrated support.

Some board members were also uneasy at the length of the statement (forty-five pages, including copious footnotes). They wished for a "more concise" document, which the CEP had rejected because of the complexity of the issues and horizon-stretching caliber of many of the concepts introduced in the proposed policy statement.

Instead of a debate on the key ideas and ethical guidelines offered in the document, the Governing Board had a three-hour procedural wrangle which never mentioned energy. In the end it was a standoff. The Governing Board issued the paper as a Study Document—an outcome that frequently consigns a report to oblivion. But at the same time the Governing Board defeated an attempt to scrap the original Committee on Energy Policy and to begin a new three-year study process under other auspices. The Committee on Energy Policy was directed to come back to the May 1979 meeting of the Governing Board with a "concise" policy statement, based on the work already done, for debate and action.*

---

*On May 11, 1979 the NCCC Governing Board (by a vote of 120 to 26, with one abstention) approved an 11-page Policy Statement on the Ethical Implications of Energy Production and Use. It essentially makes the same points as the study document condensed elsewhere in this book. The Policy Statement is available at cost from: NCCC Energy Project, Room 572, 475 Riverside Drive, New York, NY 10027. The NCCC Governing Board recommended a national energy policy in accord with the ethic of ecological justice, as follows:

An abbreviated and reorganized version of the study document, "The Ethical Implications of Energy Production and Use," follows this article. The study document highlights an ethic of ecological justice that ought to inform all education/action on the subject: "Energy has positive value only insofar as it is in harmony with the social ends of sustainability of the biosphere, equity, and participation in decision-making...." In other words, *energy is a means to desired ends, not an end in itself.* That may seem obvious, but such an ethical proposition is obscured in heated debate where values clash and organized self-interest is pitted against lack of adequate information.

Criticisms and Rejoinders

Much of what we read and hear takes for granted that "obviously, we need more energy." To back off and ask, "Wait a minute, more of what kind of energy for what use, and at what cost to whom?" is to invite immediate attack for being antitechnology and antigrowth; insensitive to the poor; utopian about alternatives; against the free market, probably socialist, perhaps anarchist; prejudiced against nuclear power; patronizing toward the Third World; and beyond the church's competence.

Many energy producers and some ethicists and other church members have leveled such charges against our study document, "Ethical Implications of Energy Production and Use." Since others

---

"We support efforts to conserve energy and to use it more efficiently.

"We support publicly funded energy-conserving projects designed in a way that will provide new skills and jobs for the unemployed.

"We support programs to limit fuel consumption that do not rely primarily on raising prices, which places an intolerable burden on the poor, the elderly and those with fixed incomes.

"We support increased Government research and development funding, subsidies and other incentives to expand the practical application of appropriate energy technologies based on renewable energy resources such as solar energy, including wind and water.

"We support a national energy policy which does not rely on a long-term large increase in the burning of coal.

"We support a national energy policy which will not need to utilize nuclear fission.

"We support a continued ban on the commercial processing and use of plutonium as a fuel in the United States, and stringent efforts to reach world-wide agreement banning such use of plutonium.

"We support the rapid development of enforceable regulations to require a social and environmental impact statement of a technology before it is widely used, and the monitoring and control of its use to prevent social and environmental damage.

"We support U.S. policy which seeks to share technologies internationally without imposing capital-intensive energy technologies on other countries.

"We support full U.S. cooperation in international efforts to ensure equitable distribution of necessary energy supplies and the rapid development and deployment of appropriate technologies based on renewable energy resources such as solar energy, including wind and water."

raising the same questions will face these perennial points of contention in the debate over energy policy, it is useful to summarize and
respond to them.

*1. Criticism: The study document is antitechnology. It rejects, or
has grave moral reservations about, some high technologies that work.
It favors unproven schemes.*

Rejoinder: The study document favors energy technologies that
support a sustainable biosphere, equitable distribution, and participation. It stresses the responsible development and use of technologies
that fit these criteria.

*2. Criticism: But you invite us to risk not having sufficient energy to
expand the economy, increase employment, and achieve a higher standard of living. We will have sufficient energy for such growth only if we
develop coal and nuclear technologies as primary sources, supplemented
by the others.*

Rejoinder: We do not have to subsidize an ever-expanding amount
of toxic energy production. The growth in energy demand can be
reduced significantly through conservation, restrictions of luxury uses
of energy, reduced advertising of energy-intensive products. Affluent
people already have sufficient energy, and are hogging it at the
expense of the poor. The study document focuses on the big risks of
ecological deterioration, unjust distribution of costs and benefits, and
lack of community involvement in energy policy-making. The last
risk suggests that we must not entrust energy policy planning to the
same corporations and regulatory agencies that brought us the crisis.

*3. Criticism: If we reduce the growth rate of energy production, a
lot of people, especially the poor, will suffer. It is much easier to meet
everyone's needs if the supply increases. To increase supply we should
develop the most available technologies as rapidly as possible, with
minimum government constraint.*

Rejoinder: Existing energy practices penalize the poor dispropor-
tionately. Low-income families already spend 30 to 50 percent of their
budget for energy (more than for any other essentials). Middle-
income families use much more, but less than 15 percent of their
income for energy expenditures. Energy policies must redress the
imbalance, so that low-income people do not have to choose between
heating and eating. We advocate special measures such as energy
stamps, lifeline utility rates, and others, and we view a national
conservation policy as beneficial to all, especially if there are public
programs and subsidies to improve existing housing stock.

The issue is not growth versus no-growth, but what kind of

growth, for whose benefit? Some forms of economic growth and increased energy production may not benefit middle- and low-income people. More nuclear power development would produce fewer jobs than would solar water heating and improved housing construction. If the present nuclear power subsidy were spent for those decentralized activities, our society would benefit considerably. Private and public funds allocated to conservation (improved insulation and weatherization of existing buildings and retrofitting them with alternative energy sources) would be the best job creators of all.

4. Criticism: We think it is unrealistic to count very much on solar technology and conservation, and we judge that both will bring more government regulation. Meanwhile, we have workable alternatives, including more oil production around the world.

Rejoinder: Many studies have shown the great job potential of conservation and solar policies. Official wisdom is beginning to catch up with the facts. The State of California estimates that manufacturing solar collectors for only one and a half million homes would result in fifty thousand jobs by 1985—more than all of California's electric and gas utilities employ today. (See Richard L. Grossman, "Energy and Employment," *Christianity and Crisis,* October 16, 1978, p. 249.) Large corporations that resist or try to discredit a primary emphasis on conservation and solar technology are reflecting their self-interest in capital-intensive, ecologically destructive technologies which do not work well economically or socially. Legislation that guarantees utilities a fixed percentage return on their capital investment obviously encourages them to continue building large-scale, centralized and expensive generating facilities. As for oil production in the developing countries, our economic and ecological woes are not solved by proliferating the importation of large quantities of oil.

5. Criticism: Fossil fuels and nuclear power give us what we want within a free-market system. The study document seems to welcome a pattern of economic planning that is socialistic.

Rejoinder: We are asking for a shift of focus in publicly funded energy research and development. Most of the research now occurs at *public expense* in thirty large corporations. We want decentralized research groups and major participation by smaller businesses. Our society has a long history of cooperative enterprises and publicly subsidized activity. What we have at present is "socialism for the rich," wherein large corporations convince the government to put up the capital and risk the liabilities of unproven energy technologies. A challenge to the concentrated power of large energy corporations offers the possibility of genuine democracy in energy policy-making and more decentralized research and development utilizing renewable resources in benign ways.

6. *Criticism: You sound like latter-day, machine-wrecking Luddites . . . or utopians who want everyone to go back to primitive farming.*

Rejoinder: Is the only alternative to the big city the primitive farm? Or a socially isolating, automobile-dependent, functionally pigeon-holing suburb? Surely our nation is not bankrupt of ingenuity and imagination to plan for a pattern of living that is environmentally safer and socially more beneficial. Of course we would have to convert some industries, and retrain those working in them, to meet new purposes. By the way, farmers are also learning techniques that are less energy- and capital-intensive, because heavily industrialized farming has begun to be unworkable.

7. *Criticism: "The Ethical Implications of Energy Production and Use" is prejudiced against nuclear power, which has an impressive safety record, and now provides 12 percent of United States electricity. We do not foresee any serious technical impediment to a solution of the waste disposal problem in the next ten years.*

Rejoinder: The government and the nuclear industry have bungled the waste-disposal problem for thirty years, and each time a solution seems near new problems become evident. Over 10 percent of the waste storage tanks have already leaked. Even though a waste processing and storage system may, eventually, be developed to a stage of reduced risks, wastes must still be transported and nuclear facilities and equipment must be "decommissioned" at high cost and with unanticipated difficulties. We reject the unproven contention of the nuclear industry that their facilities are safe for workers or for nearby residents; much more long-term health monitoring is essential to determine the dangers of low-level radiation. It is irresponsible to invest limited capital in such a toxic technology when less hazardous methods of energy production are available for development.

8. *Criticism: The study document is patronizing toward the Third World, which wants industrial development, but is offered uncertain technologies that are likely to perpetuate poverty.*

Rejoinder: The study document recognizes the dilemmas of poor countries, where higher fuel costs are much more devastating than they have been to the United States. Those countries cannot long afford to export capital through multinational enterprises and through payments for oil and nuclear technology. All countries, including poor ones, must become more energy self-sufficient, using technologies appropriate to their social structure. Most Third World countries have a large labor pool and much sunlight. Many of them are seeking ways to capitalize on these indigenous resources, but are being given little help from present United States energy research and development efforts. They do not need to repeat the massive hydro-electric errors of the 1960s with nuclear energy panaceas, which are likely to be just as inappropriate.

9. *Criticism: The NCCC study document has the overall impact of reducing church influence because it delves into technical matters beyond its competence, and it communicates a lack of faith in God's ability and our ingenuity to sustain the Creation despite human sin. It also seems in its "theological dimensions" to overstate Christian responsibility for the neighbor.*

Rejoinder: The study document encourages people to work for energy systems that are life-compatible, and to identify ethical values and criteria that make such a future possible. While expressing hope, it is not easily optimistic that, within history, God will correct all our mistakes. While God is active for justice everywhere, God does not exclude our freedom to act unjustly anywhere. God does call us to share a radical love of neighbors, whether they be near or distant in space, time, or kind. We are called to serve the poor, to care for all of creation, and to participate in the communion of saints that encompasses all generations, past and present. Failure to reform social structures and energy systems in line with these demands of our faith will accelerate political and economic anarchy and prove us unfaithful stewards.

A Glimpse of the Future

My scenario for the immediate future focuses on the plight of low-income people and our ethical task. Already, one of four is unemployed in our center cities; millions of poor and near-poor cannot meet increasing fuel and utility bills; old people and children do freeze to death because of utility cut-offs, or they succumb to disease because proper food and adequate heat are not both affordable. Many more families in this country could face severe deprivation, if not starvation, if the oil-dependent, complex food-distribution system broke down for a few weeks. Will it take riots again for the nation to comprehend the scale of desperation?

Let us be clear about the real source of chaos, and the radical forces that threaten us. It is already clear that the political left is not going to be the force that capitalizes on energy anxiety. It is the right that strongarms self-interested legislation through a feeble Congress to multiply energy profits, beats back almost every attempt to shield

the more vulnerable from the effects of the coming disaster, tries to
brainwash us to believe that somehow the profit motive is the same
thing as democracy or Christianity. If the whole thing finally falls
apart, we will have an overtly fascist government, not a new polit-
bureau.

I say *if* and not *when* because I still believe there is some space on
which to stand. When the NCCC first began to deal with plutonium
in 1975, the grounds of the debate were technical: "Is plutonium
lethal? If so, for how long? Can it be managed technologically?" Our
earlier debates saw Nobel scientists pitted against each other, with
ethicists really not on the field at all. Since then, we have moved the
debate onto the grounds where it always belonged: values, ethics,
and theology.

Today the argument is whether existing values, institutions and
vested interests will fail to bring about a sustainable, equitable and
participatory society. If they will not, then *History is not destiny . . .
the will must be found to break the momentum of habit. . . . Creation
is not static: change is coming. The church must embody Christian hope
in the fulfillment of God's gracious promise, must infuse an apprehensive
and doubting society with that hope so it will meet that challenge . . .
to bring about justice for the whole of God's creation within all of nature
and throughout all of history.*

B. NCCC Energy Study Document: "The Ethical Implications of Energy Production and Use"*

Introduction

In the midst of the intensive international debate about vanishing sources of energy and ethically acceptable means of producing and using it, humanity must make decisions which will shape societies and affect the biosphere for generations to come. Humanity is at a pivotal point. Even though the prices of petroleum and natural gas are likely to rise even further, world-wide production of these major industrial energy sources will begin to decline below present levels by the end of this century. This is the "new" energy crisis. It threatens the consumption-oriented life style of an energy-affluent elite, but will also seriously hurt the rural Third World poor.

The energy problem is a challenge to human beings who have not yet learned how equitably to distribute finite amounts of energy within biologically sustainable limits. The impact of this crisis is evident in the individual tragedy of a poor person going without food in order to pay utility bills, or a worker being without a paycheck because of interrupted coal supplies. The energy crisis is evident in

*A study document issued by the Governing Board of the National Council of Churches of Christ and commended for study by the churches. The study document has been revised and reorganized for this publication in order to highlight Christian ethical principles and to omit nonessential descriptive material and documentation.

the cultural and social destruction of a rural community by unrestrained strip mining. It is evident in the increasing desperation of two-thirds of humanity trying to survive while the remaining third consumes 83 percent of the world's commercial energy. It is evident in the plight of future generations who are to inherit deadly nuclear wastes but without adequate knowledge, technology or social institutions to deal safely with those wastes.

Energy is the capacity to do work. The work which the sun does is the operation of the biosphere. For a very long time, while many people lived at a subsistence level, the sun and human beings did the work of civilization through plants, animals, wind and water power. Since there was a clear relationship between the energy used and the end result of the completed task, the social benefits of human work were easy to assess. This assessment became more difficult as industrialized societies began to substitute complex and non-renewable energy sources—coal, petroleum, and natural gas. Most recently, as demand threatened to outgrow these sources, nuclear energy was introduced.

Complex energy technologies serve humanity and bring many benefits. Slavery might still be considered a necessary institution by some if human labor were required to do all the tasks an industrialized society demands. But these advanced technologies also have effects which cannot be so readily identified or understood. Assessing the social benefits of the work done with some of these modern energy tools is difficult. There are growing social costs involved in using these tools—in areas of health, meaningful employment and weapons proliferation, for example. It is becoming increasingly evident that other sections of society pay these social costs so that the energy demands of industrial sectors can be met. For example, burning fossil fuels produces carbon dioxide which may be affecting world weather patterns and so be turning other people's agricultural land into deserts.

The impact of modern energy technologies on society and the broader environment are much greater and last much longer than those that resulted from humanity's traditional ways of doing work. Human experience knows no precedent for these long-range effects, so there is no ready-made formula by which these technologies can be assessed. A response to the energy crisis requires not only intelligent understanding of technical data; it also requires a new set of ethical guidelines for making socially responsible choices, in an extended time-space framework, about what work should be done and which tools should be used to do it.

Energy has positive value only insofar as it is in harmony with the social ends of sustainability of the biosphere, equity, and participation in decision-making, and only insofar as its use produces valued goods which satisfy basic human needs such as food, shelter, health, and clean water and air. Human beings can now use energy technologies to sustain or to destroy life, and to alter the nature of the human species. Choices about production and use of energy are intrinsically matters of justice.

The Church's Responsibility

The energy crisis confronting society is not simply a matter of inadequate energy supply. It involves awesome burdens upon individuals, communities, nations and the whole creation. In obedience to God, Christians are called to respond to this unprecedented challenge in ways that reflect biblical understandings of creation, sin, and redemption.

From its unique perspective as a global community of believers called to protect the interests and common good of all generations, the church has a responsibility to address the ethical issues underlying the energy crisis. The church, being aware of the proper place of persons as cocreatures in the community of life, and being humbled by a clearer vision of biblical teachings about "dominion" and "stewardship," affirms the law of right relationship which is the basis of God's creation. The church is called, and calls upon society, to turn from the sin of idolizing the products of human abilities, to admit human fallibility, and to act responsibly within the finitude of creation.

All persons are called by God to care for each other, especially for the poor and powerless, and to care for the living space of present and future generations. Because all human beings are made in God's image, all persons are called to work together in a common human commitment to the ethic of ecological justice.

A faithful response to such a challenge will require prayerful searching for guidance to make necessary changes in the individual life styles of Christians, in the institutional life styles of our churches, and in the corporate life styles of our societies. A faithful response will require that Christians obtain the knowledge needed to participate responsibly in communal decisions which can help to shape an ecologically just society. A faithful response will require changes in present structures and decision-making processes which impede the attainment of such a society. A faithful response from Christians in the scientific and technical disciplines will require that they understand

and apply the ethic of ecological justice in their work, in order to develop energy technologies that do not themselves violate the values of sustainability, equity and participation.

A Definition of Ecological Justice

The ethic of ecological justice means equity for all members of the community of life within the sustainable boundaries of the biosphere. Ecology has its roots in the Greek word, *oikos*, which means "home," while the Latin root of justice means "what is right and fair." Ecological justice is an ethic of wholeness. There are no isolated victims on a small planet; without ecological justice, all are potential victims.

The ethic of ecological justice provides guidelines for human choice and action. An ecologically just society will be guided by the values of sustainability, equity, and participation.

Sustainability refers to the earth's limited capacity to provide resources and to absorb the pollution resulting from their use. Sustainability requires that biological and social systems which nurture and support life be neither depleted nor poisoned. Sustainability provides the boundaries within which all participate in the equitable satisfaction of needs.

Equity refers to a fair distribution of resources on the basis of need. Equity embodies the rights of today's generation and those yet unborn. A central concern of energy policy is the equitable distribution of positive and negative impacts of energy production and use. This distribution is difficult because what is beneficial to one group of people often is detrimental to another; because frequently those who receive the benefits are not those who pay the costs; and because there is a considerable time lag between the imposition of either costs or benefits and the realization of long-term effects. Energy equity questions include: Energy for whom? Energy for how long and for what? How much and what kind of energy?

Participation is a basis of equity in that the individual community member must have the opportunity to be involved in determining public policy and the hierarchy of values which guide that policy. Participation includes representation of the interests of future generations.

Ecological justice is an ethic of means as well as an ethic of ends. *In order to achieve the end of an ecologically just society, the means themselves must be ecologically just.*

Evaluating Risks Within Ecological Boundaries

All energy technologies involve risk. However, errors by today's decision-makers on the use of some energy technologies could commit future generations to irreversible conditions of catastrophe. While past generations have inherited conditions of irreversible ecological damage, those catastrophes were never global in nature.

The wide range of risks associated with energy production and use may be ranked on a "scale of severity" from acceptable to unacceptable. Some risks may be judged unacceptable.

In the case of technologies which threaten the possibility of irreversible global damage, a major ethical question is whether it is fair for the present generation to reap the benefits while future generations bear the cost.

Modern energy technologies also increase the number of both voluntary and involuntary risks to which individuals and society are exposed. *Preferable technologies would allow for the lowest degree of involuntary risk.* This implies that preferable technologies are those which people can understand and about which information is readily available.

High-risk Technologies

Risks are a major consideration in the evaluation of suitable substitutes for oil and gas. For example, consider the choice to commit the United States to a long-range (beyond the year 2000) coal- or nuclear fission-based energy policy. If the coal option is chosen, there is the certainty of an increase in black lung disease among coal miners and of cancer among people exposed to polluted air. Burning more coal could also result in less certain but irreversible climatic damage from increased carbon dioxide in the atmosphere. Changes in climate can turn agricultural land into deserts.

If the nuclear fission option is chosen, there is increased probability of cancer among uranium miners, of biological and social hazards of waste storage hundreds of centuries into the future, and of radioactive release caused by nuclear war and/or nuclear accident. Preventive security measures throughout the nuclear fuel cycle—from fuel transportation to long-term waste storage—require extraordinary vigilance.

Human fallibility, democratic institutions and preservation of life and world peace are values which should be included in criteria for risk assessment. On the basis of these criteria, the use of plutonium technologies poses an unacceptable risk.

Plutonium is a potential fuel for the next generation of nuclear fission plants, liquid metal fast-breeder reactors. It can also be recovered from the spent nuclear fuel and reused in this generation of power plants. Plutonium is "fiendishly toxic." A small amount can produce cancer; it can also be used to fashion nuclear weapons. A plutonium-based economy will involve the handling and transporting of large amounts of plutonium. Because of the grave nature of the threat to life and world peace, a plutonium-based economy would require accident-free performance by machines and by human beings.

Given these conditions, plutonium is not a fuel appropriate to the dimensions of human nature. Human beings are fallible and capable of error. The authoritarian institutions which would be necessary to isolate plutonium from the environment are antithetical to democracy and a threat to civil liberties. These institutions and energy tools would be an inappropriate legacy for future generations.

In seeking substitutes for oil and gas, there are many other energy options, all involving risks. Some electricity-generating solar technologies may remove large areas of land from agricultural use. The challenge of conservation involves allocating energy on the basis of equity—which may risk limiting individual freedoms, a difficult program in a democracy—and meeting the capital costs of materials and redesign of industrial processes. However, these risks do not threaten irreversible harm; they do seem to balance risks and benefits more fairly. Solar energy and conservation allow for greater measures of voluntary rather than involuntary risk for both today's and future generations, without severe negative impact on political institutions.

It is an ethical imperative to recognize when human ability to assess risks and to predict the likelihood of actual harm is not equal to the enormity of possible consequences of human action. In the absence of knowledge and faced by possible catastrophe, it is appropriate to recommend prudence and caution. Equity points to a guiding principle: *future generations should not be placed at risk for the benefit of the present generation.*

One of the major problems an ethical energy policy must address is the possibility that without a substantial commitment to high-risk energy sources there will be insufficient supply. Clearly there are some risks which should not be taken. Recent developments have increased concern about the use of both coal and nuclear fission, and have provided the basis for greater optimism about the technological and social possibilities of solar energy.

Guidelines for Technology Assessment

A guiding ethic for assessing technological risks should be the preservation of options: "Other things being equal, those technological projects or developments should be favored that leave maximum room for maneuver in the future. The reversibility of an action should thus be counted as a major benefit; its irreversibility a major cost."

This guideline has the added attraction of allowing for the possibility of technological breakthroughs which, if socially desirable, could be added to the energy mix.

A stringent conservation policy is necessary both to avoid commitment to technologies involving unacceptable risks and to support society through a transition period from oil and gas to ecologically sustainable substitutes. It is unconscionable for some persons to waste energy when others now and in the future will bear the costs. The costs are rising in food, as agriculture becomes more energy-dependent, and in international stability, as developed countries export military hardware to pay for oil.

There is no doubt that, like high-risk energy options, the solar/conservation/innovation response will involve social and economic trade-offs and some curtailment of freedom. Conservation and redistribution of resources will require decisions by national and international bodies that may inhibit the freedom to waste enjoyed by smaller social groups and some individuals. But freedom may also be enhanced by relieving dependency on centralized, complex and high-risk technologies. The locus of decision-making for less complex technologies may be decentralized. *The process of anticipating serious threats to the quality of life posed by energy technologies must include technology assessment and social impact assessment.*

Technology assessment would favor technology which is consistent with as many as possible of the following criteria:

a) resilient: capable of absorbing shocks (e.g., oil embargoes, severe winters) without major social disruptions;

b) flexible: capable of timely change during development and utilization in order to adapt to unpredictable events;

c) pluralistic: assuring a diversity of options, life styles and opportunities;

d) noncentralizing: encouraging a scale that permits choice and control by the user;

e) benign: protective of the human and natural environment;

f) inequity-reducing: allocating benefits and costs to all on a more equitable basis;

g) nonviolent: difficult to use directly or indirectly as a weapon;

h) resource-saving: providing satisfactory services with minimal resources and maximum results;

i) practical: capable of being used for safe, fulfilling work processes;

j) aesthetic: pleasing to the senses;

k) simple: achieving a sophisticated economy of means in a manner understandable to the user.

Social impact assessment would require establishing a scale of impacts from acceptable to unacceptable which would distinguish between short- and long-term effects. Social impact assessment would address at least the areas of community development and cohesion, employment, industry development, land use, health and community services. Careful social impact assessments must be made to judge the effects of energy production and use on satisfaction of physical needs like food, health, water and shelter, and of spiritual and aesthetic needs.

Assessments may indicate that significantly increased amounts of energy will improve the quality of life for some by satisfying unmet basic needs. For others, an increase in energy may lower the quality of life. What is good for one nation or group of persons may not be good for another. Although the individual material standard of living of the rich may decline, the overall quality of life may be improved. *A guiding principle should be that meeting the needs of all persons must take priority over satisfying the wants of any.*

Toward Equity and Participation

Mechanisms for equitable energy distribution should be institutionalized, and energy growth targeted to the poor. Given the reality of a postabundant world, in which there will *not* be "more for everyone," equity points to a guiding principle: the needs of those who are below the minimum standard of need take precedence. Since survival depends on it, energy should be allocated on a standard that insures adequate food, health, housing, and clean air and water for all.

Since energy is necessary to survival, the poor must be guaranteed adequate supplies. Equity guidelines suggest the need for consideration, in the United States, of energy stamps and utility rate reforms such as lifelining. Rationing of oil should be considered, rather than relying only on high prices to limit its consumption.

Public money should be effectively allocated to increase the energy efficiency of the poor through winterization and insulation of homes. The poor, both urban and rural, could benefit from participation in the development of new energy technologies which are labor-intensive and require low capital and basic skills. Neighborhood-based heating installations, insulation programs, roof-top solar panels and other community-based technologies are well-suited to small-scale business development. These technologies could be the basis for job-training programs and provide opportunities for previously excluded groups to enter the energy business. Broad participation in energy policy considerations will widen responsibility for decision-making. *An ethic of participation points to a guiding principle: the views of those who will be affected by a particular action ought to be considered.*

Protection of Different Cultures

It is important to protect the religious freedom, cultural integrity and habitat of racial and ethnic minorities. Not long ago, it was planned to construct six gigantic coal-burning electricity plants and three huge strip mines at and around Black Mesa, Arizona. The electrical power was to be distributed to distant urban areas. The health risks and water and air pollution would be distributed to Native American communities, six major national parks and twenty-eight national monuments.

Black Mesa is the ancestral home of the Hopi and Navajo nations and is considered sacred by many of them. This planned sacrifice of spiritual shrines has been described as "ripping apart St. Peter's in order to sell the marble." Many Native Americans value the earth as Mother, in contrast to the pervasive American attitude which identifies mastery of the earth with "progress." What value should be placed on a culture, a religion, or an irreplaceable natural area?

Boomtown Problems

Rural communities situated in areas of abundant energy resources in the western United States are today having their resources developed by companies which have no long-term interest in the local culture and economy. The experience of these communities is reminiscent of Appalachia and of the economic and cultural domination so well documented in the experiences of many developing countries. Too large a percentage of the profits from resource development is exported rather than invested locally. Communities are often left with inadequate financial resources to sustain themselves through the impact period or to invest in alternate forms of livelihood when mineral resources are depleted. The social fabric of the community collapses and the local economy goes from boom to bust.

The permanent population affected by the boomtown syndrome is much smaller than the large urban population which uses the energy. Yet values of equity and participation support the right of minorities to some measure of self-determination. *Social impact assessment should precede development, and the data should be made available to local citizens.* These assessments, like risk, should be based on intelligible general criteria, by which significant impacts can be identified and ranked on a scale of severity. When impacts of energy development threaten necessary local resources, such as water, they may be judged unacceptable. Although impact assessments and decisions on energy development involve the interests and expertise of a variety of groups, local citizens have a right and a responsibility to participate in them. Those who will directly benefit from the energy—often distant urban areas and energy corporations—have a responsibility to ameliorate those impacts. Urban areas should move toward greater energy efficiency and conservation, and corporations toward increased payment of local revenues and social audits of their activities.

Equity and Conservation

The United States, with 5.8 percent of the world's population, consumes 33 percent of the world's commercial energy. It is estimated that about half of this energy could eventually be saved by more efficient use. Therefore, American citizens must ask what changes in individual and corporate life styles are needed to reduce energy consumption with minimal social and economic dislocation.

Reluctance to reduce energy use is often based on the assumption that there is a rigid coupling between energy use and a high material standard of living, as measured by the Gross National Product (GNP). This assumption has been challenged by research that shows a high degree of variability in the relationship between GNP and energy use, depending on regions, countries, prices and life styles.

The United States is now identifying changes in energy use which might reduce consumption. High fuel prices and threatened shortages have already led cost-conscious businesses to institute significant conservation measures, such as reducing unnecessary office lighting and adopting energy-saving industrial processes. Government regulations promise other savings, as in requirements for lower fuel consumption by new automobiles. Many citizens have turned down heat and air-conditioning, had their gas-stove pilot lights shut off and have switched to car pools.

Continuing education and information about the necessity of and practical methods to save energy are needed 'for willing public participation. Increasing research and development should be directed to innovative conservation techniques. *Public funds should be used to stimulate employment opportunities in conservation programs*, such as raising energy efficiency in existing and new buildings. Legal and regulatory adjustments are needed to encourage many conservation measures, such as recycling of materials.

Conservation guidelines include matching the kind of energy to the work to be done. For instance, it makes sense to use electricity to run subways or communications, and to replace electricity with solar energy to heat water and homes. Another guideline is to assess the amount of energy used to manufacture a product, not just the amount needed to run it.

Given the will of institutions and individuals to practice conservation, it could become a major United States energy resource. It is much cheaper and less depleting not to use energy than to produce it.

Equity and Third World Energy Needs

Over one hundred developing nations are striving for rapid economic growth. They hope for and need a large portion of the world's diminishing energy resources. Eighty of these nations are nonexporters of petroleum; twenty-seven are the poorest in the world. On the basis of a standard of need, how can the rich countries help the poor to meet their goals?

The international community must give priority consideration to the particular vulnerability of developing countries most dependent on oil to satisfy their essential agricultural, industrial and economic requirements. The success of international oil conservation measures depends largely on the success of the United States in reducing oil imports. For us this implies serious and even severe conservation measures and innovative development of safe domestic energy sources.

Third World countries must play a full role in research and policy decisions which will affect their energy futures. Research and development efforts should be directed to exploration and production of appropriate energy resources and their use within developing countries. Increased reforestation would aid the 80 to 90 percent of the rural populations of Africa, Asia and Latin America who rely on wood for fuel. Comparatively small-scale regional electric generating plants are needed, since production from large centralized plants does not meet the needs of the majority of the people, who live in rural areas. Massive unemployment in many countries indicates the need for labor-intensive industrial development.

There has been considerable debate over the role of nuclear energy in meeting Third World needs. Such large-scale facilities are frequently inappropriate for their economies. The complex technology and high capital investment required to build and operate nuclear plants leads developing countries into even more dependency on foreign and transnational energy companies and foreign banks or governments.

Most Third World countries are located in regions where solar energy is abundant; many of them are island nations or have ocean boundaries. These characteristics indicate the need for development of technologies which can utilize the bountiful diversity of these nations, such as solar, tidal, and ocean-thermal energy. Developing these technologies as major energy sources will take time, and should begin immediately.

Conclusion

The goal of a sustainable, equitable and participatory energy policy is energy sufficiency for all. To reach this goal will require stringent conservation by the affluent, especially in the use of oil and petroleum products, and a strong commitment to the development of renewable energy resources, especially solar energy, and to social and technological innovation.

A stringent conservation policy is necessary both to avoid unacceptable risks and to sustain industrialized society through a transition period from oil and gas to ecologically sustainable substitutes. It is unconscionable for some persons to waste energy when others now and in the future will bear the costs.

An energy policy designed in the public interest will limit risks, allocate energy more equitably, assess and limit the impacts of technologies and move to an ethic of sharing. Christians are challenged to join with all persons of integrity and good will in shaping an ecologically just society. Such a society will respect the limits of creation—the fallibility of human beings, the finite supply of resources, the inability of the natural world endlessly to absorb unnatural substances, and the reality that everything and everyone is connected with every other thing and every other one in the community of life.

Such a society will respond to the demands of equitable distribution by ensuring that finite resources are thoughtfully conserved so that they may be equitably shared to meet the needs of all persons, now and in the future. Such a society will ensure that satisfaction of human needs takes immediate priority over the satisfaction of anyone's desires, and that the dignity of each individual is honored by providing opportunity for all persons to participate responsibly in decisions which will affect their individual lives and the common good.

Appendix A

Theological Dimensions of the Energy Situation

by William H. Lazareth*

Creation

Creation is portrayed in the scriptures as an ongoing activity that demonstrates God's sovereign power and love. God creates and preserves the world so that everything in it is purposefully interrelated with everything else. Life is created and work is enabled through the continuous cosmic transformation of energy. All organic and inorganic components of massive ecological systems are dynamically interconnected. This miraculous creation is declared by God to be good precisely in its universal interconnectedness.

Human beings are made by God as persons-in-nature, cocreatures in reciprocal relationship with everything else that God made. As an integral part of creation, humanity shares in the finite nature of that creation. Persons cannot hope to live their lives apart from or in opposition to the interconnectedness of humanity and the rest of God's creatures.

Only after making the basic affirmation that the creatureliness of human beings is shared with the rest of creation does the Bible declare that humans are distinctive because they are created in God's image.

*Director, Department of Church and Society, Division for Mission in North America, Lutheran Church in America.

Persons are unique in their capacity to respond to God with faith, to their human neighbors with love, and to the nonhuman part of creation with respect and responsible care.

The Old Testament declares that an essential part of the divine commission to humanity is to exercise "dominion" over the earth and to "till and keep it." The obedient fulfillment of God's mandate calls for humans to think and work together both as accountable stewards of the whole earth and as bold advocates for fairness and freedom in the human community. This means that all persons, since they are created in God's image, are responsible for the wise conservation of the Creator's gift of limited energy in order to achieve a more just, sustainable and participatory society for today and for the future.

Sin

Humanity has often selfishly distorted the divine commission to exercise dominion into an unlimited license to exploit the material world and weaker persons. This perversion of dominion into domination is a sin and it is one of the underlying causes of the energy crisis. Sin is rebellion against God. When faith in the Creator is replaced by faith in human ability to solve all problems by technical means, humanity has fallen into the sin of idolatry. From this perspective, sin may be understood as willful transgression of the laws of right relationship which God built into the creation. This right relationship may be characterized by the Hebrew word *Shalom,* meaning wholeness, peace and justice in community. By seeking to serve only ourselves instead of serving God and our fellow-creatures, we forsake our true humanity as responsible and relational beings in nature, created in the image of God. The current energy situation can be seen as the result of the idolatrous and unjust ways in which humans have used, abused, or neglected to use the limited sources of energy the Creator has made available for the well-being of the continuing creation.

Idolatry

In the Old Testament, idolatry is condemned by the Hebrew prophets as one of the chief ways in which individuals and their created institutions violate the laws of right relationship. The concept of idolatry is particularly helpful in understanding modern abuses of energy and technology. Idolatry is the perversion of our relationship to God, placing distorted trust for our salvation in other sources of power. While these sources may be properly used in obedience to

God's will, such distortion transforms them into false idols. In ancient
Israel, the powers of creativity were often perverted into idols of
nature gods and fertility goddesses to be worshipped. Today, human
intelligence and labor and their products, as embodied in science and
technology, are often elevated into similar counterfeit deities, which
must be served even at the sacrifice of individual and corporate well-
being.

Injustice

The sin of idolatry supports the sin of domination. Increasing
domination of humans over nature results in the increasing domination of some humans and their institutions over others. Technological
systems tend to become instruments of economic and political domination.

Current world-wide inequities of wealth and power reflect a
situation of injustice in human society. This sinful condition was
continuously condemned by the prophets of God, who called upon
the rich and powerful to divest themselves of their unjustly accumu-
lated wealth so that the poor and powerless could receive their share
of the earth's resources. The Bible makes clear that the fertility of the
earth—its ability to sustain human life in *Shalom*—is intimately
bound up with the protection of justice in the social order.*

Redemption

There are a variety of ways in which people seek to meet the threat
to human survival posed by the energy crisis and its origin in human
injustice. Christians will find in the Gospel of Jesus Christ their
ultimate hope for the fulfillment of God's gracious promises. God
has redeemed us by the crucifixion and resurrection of Christ,
incorporated us into Christ's body, the church, and called us to loving
service in the world. Liberated by the love of Christ and empowered
by the Holy Spirit, Christians witness to God's inbreaking reign by
participating in the ongoing struggle for justice and human rights. In
individual life styles and through responsible management of corporate complexities, Christians engage in this struggle, not out of a love
of power, but by the power of God's love for the whole of creation.
In Christ, we are freed from preoccupation with our own rights and
needs so that we can give ourselves to the securing of justice for our
neighbors in their need.

---

*Psalm 72; Lev. 26:18-20; Hosea 4:2-3; Isa. 24:4 ff.

All Are Neighbors in the Community of Life

"Who is my neighbor?" Jesus Christ asked in his day. In the Parable of the Good Samaritan, he dramatically expanded the meaning of neighbor current among his contemporaries by breaking down the traditional barriers of culture, race, and religion. However, this newly expanded definition still referred only to other living human beings.

Prompted by the energy crisis, people are again asking, with increasing urgency, "Who is my neighbor?" Spectacular advances in modern technology are helping increasing numbers of people to understand that within the interconnectedness of creation, all are neighbors. A new vision of cosmic discipleship is emerging as we are called to explore the ultimate physical and temporal boundaries of the community of life.

An Ethic of Ecological Justice

Our understanding of neighbor is now being radically expanded to encompass all humans in past, present and future generations, as well as the rest of creation. The Bible has always insisted that human faithlessness and injustice could destroy the creation. The expanded effects in time and space of human actions enabled by advanced technology make our responsibility inescapable. Human responsibility for future generations cannot be adequately met with an ethic that deals only with the rights of human beings who are presently alive. We are called to embrace an ethic that takes into moral consideration the claims of those involved and endangered neighbors who, in the present energy debate, are necessarily voiceless because they do not yet exist, or because they exist in the nonhuman creation.

Ecological justice is such an ethic. It is an ethic for all members of the community of life, inspired by Christian hope for the fulfillment of God's promises. To be faithful to its calling, the Church of Jesus Christ must advocate justice for the whole of God's creation within all of nature and throughout all of history.

The Biblical Promise

Saint Paul bore witness to responsible freedom within the mysterious interconnectedness between the realms of nature and history in God's good earth when he said, "For the creation waits with eager longing for the revealing of the [children] of God; for the creation was subjected to futility, not of its own will but by the will of [the one] who subjected it in hope; because the creation itself will be set free from its bondage to decay and obtain the glorious liberty of the children of God." (Rom. 8:19-21)

Chart 8

"NEIGHBORS" IN BIBLICAL PERSPECTIVE

NOW	IN THE FUTURE
HUMAN BEINGS ALIVE	
THE REST OF CREATION	

Appendix B

Individual/Institutional Conservation

Energy Intensive Activities

The total energy and labor intensity of the twenty activities of personal consumption expenditures (PCE) which are highest in terms of dollars. Ranked in order of decreasing energy intensity. Numbers in parentheses are for aggregated activities. 1971.

Chart 9

ACTIVITY	ENERGY INTENSITY —BTUs	LABOR INTENSITY —Jobs (Hundred Thousand $)
Electricity	502,500	4.4
Gasoline and oil	480,700	7.3
(Housing)	(144,000)	(N/A)
(Auto Ownership)	(111,500)	(8.1)
Cleaning preparations	78,100	7.3
(Average for all personal consumption)	(70,000)	(8.0)
Kitchen and household appliances	58,700	5.5
New and used cars	55,600	7.8
Other durable house furniture	54,600	8.9

(Private investment)	(45,600)	(6.6)
Food purchases	41,100	8.5
Furniture	36,700	9.2
(Federal spending)	(36,300)	(8.2)
Women's and children's clothing	33,100	10.0
Restaurants	32,400	8.8
Men's and boys' clothing	31,400	9.8
Religious and welfare activity	27,800	8.5
Private hospitals	26,100	17.2
Automobile repair and maintenance	23,500	4.8
Financial interests except insurance	21,500	7.8
Tobacco products	19,800	5.8
Telephone and telegraph	19,000	5.9
Rented home (interest plus some utilities)	18,300	3.5
Physicians	10,700	3.3
Own home (interest charges only)	8,300	1.7

From: Bruce M. Hannon, *Energy Growth and Altruism*, an unpublished manuscript, University of Illinois at Champaign/Urbana, Center for Advanced Computation.

A Personal Conservation Guide*

Energy conservation is the most important and the most ignored facet of energy policy. A vigorous conservation program will permit us to bridge the next twenty-five years without becoming hooked on either hazardous energy technologies or unreliable sources of supply. Energy conservation will make more net energy available per dollar spent than any other energy supply option, and will allow us to minimize the environmental degradation associated with all current energy production technologies. A strong national conservation program can contribute to human wealth, create employment opportunities, and lead to a more stable and sustainable national economy.

Conscientious individuals can take some basic steps to conserve energy. Six such simple actions are listed below.

1. Make gasoline mileage your paramount concern in purchasing a new car. Oversized cars, over-powered engines, automatic transmissions, and unnecessary power options should be avoided.

2. Bicycle or walk to work if possible. If not, use public transportation, join a car pool, or urge your employer to establish a van pool.

*Denis Hayes, *Energy: The Case for Conservation* (Worldwatch Institute, Paper 4, January, 1976), pp. 65-70.

For long or short trips, always use the most energy-efficient mode and route of travel compatible with your time schedule.

3. Make sure your dwelling has ample insulation. For many home owners, house insulation will provide a higher rate-of-return through fuel savings than any other available investment. In addition, it will increase the value of your property.

4. When purchasing appliances and other power equipment, always buy the most energy-efficient brand and model. Most popular consumer publications now examine the relative energy efficiencies of products.

5. Reduce the lighting within your control by using smaller light bulbs, avoiding excessive lighting, and turning off all unnecessary lights.

6. If at all possible, plant a home garden. A carefully tended 20' by 20' plot can produce $400 worth of fresh produce, saving both fuel and money. If you live in an apartment, urge your management to set aside some outdoor space for resident gardens.

Note: Although energy efficiency is of enormous importance, no activity should be judged nor social choice made solely on the basis of the fuel consumption involved. In addition to energy husbandry, we have a great many goals to consider and balance. A more energy-intensive expenditure might help maintain or enhance social equity, physical beauty, or national security. Extra energy can speed up a construction project or shave ten minutes from a commuter's travel time. Often speed is a convenience; occasionally it is a necessity. A doctor who has the option of rushing to an accident in a car, a bus, a train, or on a bicycle is not necessarily wasting energy by using a car.

Individual actions, though necessary, are not sufficient. A strong national conservation program will come about only if demanded by an aroused and informed citizenry. The time has come to press our political representatives to change the rules of the game in ways that promote energy conservation—to eliminate tax incentives that encourage the consumption of fuel and other virgin resources, transport rates that discriminate against recycled goods, and utility rate structures that reward energy gluttony.

Policy-makers and consumers alike must learn to recognize the following broad categories of energy conservation strategies: prices, taxes, allocations, incentives, regulations, and exhortation.

1. *Prices* and *taxes* both work to make a source of energy more expensive to the consumer. If the price of gasoline rises rapidly, due

to market forces or to increasing taxes, consumers will buy less gasoline.

2. *Allocations* place floors and ceilings on the amount of fuel available to each consumer through, for example, coupon rationing and fuel lifelines.

3. *Incentives* provide the consumer with a positive reward for using less energy. Tax breaks may be offered to homeowners who insulate or to businesses that adopt more energy-efficient processes.

4. *Regulations* take the form of simple legal requirements and prohibitions. Federal legislation could mandate a minimum mileage standard for automobiles, and building codes could be expanded to require strict insulation standards.

5. *Exhortation* is the proclamation of the economic and other advantages of conservation; it ensures that the public is well-informed, and creates a climate of opinion in which energy conservation is seen as desirable and worthwhile. This category encompasses such diverse actions as public education commercials and appliance efficiency labels.

Many conservation programs will involve elements of each of these strategies. The importance of an effective combination cannot be exaggerated. Where there's no will, there's no way.

Steps for the Congregation*

The energy consumption of many public buildings can be cut by as much as 30 percent without a major investment of capital or labor. These savings could easily mount to $1000 or $2000 a year for a small-to-medium church in the middle and northern latitudes.

The overwhelming majority of the 330,000 religious buildings that dot the American landscape can be accurately described as energy sieves. Frequently, the structures are poorly insulated and improperly designed for meaningful energy conservation. The most glaring problem is heat loss. Furnaces must labor to warm vast spaces that are never occupied, such as the upper reaches of the sanctuary or nave. On many occasions, an entire church plant is heated up to accommodate a board meeting of twenty people or to keep the office area warm during the week.

To be sure, the opportunities for energy conservation may be limited in cathedral-type structures with high ceilings and extensive glazing. It must also be acknowledged that certain conservation measures (e.g., combustion-control systems, thermal storage units,

---

*Prepared by the Interfaith Coalition on Energy, 1757 S Street, NW, Washington, DC 20009.

stack gas recovery systems, etc.) may be beyond the financial reach of many congregations. Nevertheless, a significant number of synagogues and churches could be effectively insulated for as little as $1000. The resultant savings in fuel costs could pay back the congregation's investment within one or two years. Other conservation measures requiring little or no front money include lower thermostat settings, caulking, weatherstripping, self-closing doors, avoidance of electric space heaters, protective yard plantings, and the use of thermal window barriers. Parishioners should also consider solar hotwater heating, currently competitive with electricity in most parts of the country.

In addition to church buildings, many clerical residences are also overdue for major conservation measures. A combination of insulation, storm windows and doors, caulking, and weatherstripping in these homes can reduce fuel consumption by half. The potential for savings is even greater when a package of conservation features is built into new homes (e.g., continuous vapor barriers, specially placed windows, lined air ducts, wide stud spacings, solar space heating.

The checklist that follows presents a range of options for conserving energy. Some of these would require only marginal adjustments in the operation or structure of a building, while others would have a major impact on the congregation. Certain measures might be effective only if specific conditions were met (e.g., heat pumps are most useful in areas where winters are mild). Most of the suggestions on this list can also be applied to clerical residences. Limited capital loan funds for church clergy conservation projects may be available from your denominational headquarters or regional office.

*Conservation Checklist**
Chart 10

PROBLEM AREAS	ENERGY CONSERVING MEASURES
thermostat setting	50° on weekdays, 65° on sabbath
drafts	weatherstripping, caulking, self-closing doors
outdoor building exposure ...	barrier walls and plantings on northern and western sides, deciduous trees on the south

---

*Prepared by Interfaith Coalition on Energy, 1757 "S" Street, N.W., Washington, D.C. 20009.

window heat loss	double-glazing, clear glass, replacement of broken glass, thermal barriers (drapes, banners, or movable frames of polyethylene for placement over windows at night)
congregational attitudes	sermons and educational programs on energy conservation, creation of psychological warmth (candles, bright colors, banners, cushions)
heating of church office	use of clerical residence for study
weekday heating of plant ...	sharing of building with other groups (day care centers, community clinics, art galleries, other congregations)
heating of cavernous .... worship areas	setting up of chapel in another part of building, insulated drop (false) ceilings, insulated partitions, modular heating (heating of small area only)
cold attics	insulation (batts, blankets, loose fill)
hot water heaters	insulation jackets, pipe insulation, solar water heaters
poor furnace efficiency	regular maintenance, oil additive for oil fired systems, heat pumps, packaged heating systems
summer cooling	fans and proper ventilation, dehumidifiers, avoidance of central air conditioning, early morning/late evening meetings, use of basement or inner rooms
new building design	proper site utilization (maximized southern exposure, use of protective plantings, etc.), compact floor plan, sun shades and overhangs, low ceilings, heavily insulated attics and walls, modular heating capacity, simple solar systems for space and water heating, adjoining greenhouses for heat and community food production
lighting	sodium lamps, rheostats, clear glass for natural lighting, fluorescent lights (four times as efficient as incandescent, seven to ten times the lifetime of incandescent, lower operating cost)

Appendix C

Use Energy Resource Projection

Chart 11

Resource	Energy Quads		
	1977	1990	2000
Nuclear fission	3	5	3
Petroleum	30	26	15
Natural gas	25	20	15
Coal/shale	15	15	10
Syncrude	—	2	5
Syngas	—	3	5
Hydro	2	3	3
Geothermal	—	2	5
Solar thermal	—	3	12
Solar electric	—	0.5	3
Biomass	—	8	15
Ocean thermal	—	0.5	3
Wind	—	2	6
Total	75	90	100
Centralized systems (> $100M)	75	73.5	65
Carbon-based resources	70	65	66
Decentralized systems	0	16.5	35

July 9, 1978. NM. C. G. Currin (a participant in Ghost Ranch Conference on Energy Ethics, Abiquiu, NM)

Appendix D

Other Ways To Go*

There is nothing fundamentally new about these energy resources. Most people in the world rely on them for their energy needs. What is new are various technologies and methods enabling their use in industrial societies as major energy resources.

Solar

In half a day, the United States receives the same amount of energy from the sun that it consumes for all purposes in an entire year.

In 1952, the Paley Commission reported to President Truman that with a concerted effort begun then, 13 million homes and commercial buildings could be heated by solar energy by 1975. The reasons why that goal was never achieved were political rather than technical. The vast resources for energy development were committed to nuclear power.

Carter's energy plan called for 2.5 million homes heated by solar resources by 1985. Secretary of Energy Schlesinger later reduced that to 1.3 million.

*Reprinted from *Sojourners* 7, no. 6 (1978). *Sojourners*, 1309 L Street N.W., Washington, D.C. 20005.

There are two general forms of solar energy, passive and active. Passive solar energy for heating works on the same principle as leaving your car shut with the windows up on a sunny day: the temperature inside increases. Homes and buildings can be designed in ways to maximize the use of this free energy.

Active solar systems use cells to trap the sun's energy for purposes such as heating homes and hot water. Such systems cost about what electrical heating systems cost today, and studies for the government have concluded that solar systems can compete with oil and natural gas in five years. With development and expanded use, the price of solar energy drops, while the price of oil, natural gas, and nuclear-powered electricity continues to rise. The local price of conventional energy resources, rather than the number of sunny days, is the chief factor determining the present competitiveness of solar energy in any region of the country.

Initial investment costs for solar heating systems often make them seem far more expensive than they are. The amount of time that bills for fuel oil, gas, or electricity equal the cost of a solar system grows shorter every time the price of those resources increases. A few states, such as California, have adopted tax credits as one way to offset the present initial cost of installing solar systems.

Today there are no more than sixty thousand homes in the United States with solar hot water heaters. In Israel there are 200,000; in Japan there are two million.

Photovoltaic Cells

The sun's energy can be turned directly into electricity through photovoltaic cells. Many cameras with automatic electric eyes use this solar electricity. The high cost of these cells at present makes the electricity they produce far more expensive than other options.

But a report for the Federal Energy Administration last year indicated that if the government would buy such solar equipment in large quantities for its own use, that would make photovoltaic cells affordable on a widespread basis in five years. Such an investment would be equal to no more than one-half the cost of a single nuclear power plant.

Wind

Six million windmills have been built in the United States, and 150,000 still run today.

A variety of innovative experiments is being undertaken to harness the wind's power for energy needs. Some, including several by major energy companies, seem expensive and impractical. But others are promising.

In the Texas Panhandle, a region with a vast potential for wind energy, demonstration projects using wind to facilitate in producing electricity for irrigation pumps are underway. In Denmark, a college built a 2,000-kilowatt wind turbine for $660,000 or $330 per kilowatt. That is cheaper than just the cost of fuel for an oil-powered electrical generating plant, to say nothing of the cost of building such a facility.

And in New York City, a windmill put up by imaginative innovators on an apartment building not only generated electricity for their use, but made Con Ed's meter run backwards, putting electricity back into its system.

Biomass

The largest untapped potential energy source in New York City today may well be its garbage. Wastes from both cities and farms and even sewage all contain unused energy which can be recovered. A few cities are doing just that, burning solid wastes to create the steam for generating electricity.

A company in Texas is taking animal dung and freeing the methane—natural gas—it contains, putting it in a pipeline to the Midwest. That same principle is used throughout the Third World, where biogas plants in a local home or village take animal and human wastes to produce energy for running a refrigerator, operating an irrigation pump, cooking food or other purposes. China has built 4.3 million such biogas plants. There are 100 in the United States.

Wood wastes can produce fuel for vehicles as well. Brazil plans to run all its cars on ethanol, produced by burning sugar cane and other wood wastes, by the end of the century.

NOTES

Chapter 1: Eco-Justice in the Eighties

1. Amory B. Lovins, "The Soft Energy Path," *The Center Magazine,* XI, 5 (September-October 1978), pp. 32 ff.

2. For an overview of energy producer concerns, cf. Carol and John Steinhart, *The Fires of Culture: Energy Yesterday and Tomorrow.* (North Scituate, Mass.: Duxbury Press, 1974), pp. 219-30.

3. Herman E. Daly, "Energy Demand Forecasting: Prediction or Planning?" *AIP Journal* (January 1976), p. 12.

4. Cf. Dieter T. Hessel, *A Social Action Primer* (Philadelphia: Westminster Press, 1972), p. 75.

5. Cf. Robert Jewett and John Shelton Laurence, *The American Monomyth* (Garden City, N.Y.: Doubleday, Anchor Press, 1977).

6. Denis Hayes, *Energy: The Case for Conservation* (Worldwatch Institute, Paper 4, January 1976), pp. 7-11.

7. William E. Gibson, "The Lifestyle of Christian Faithfulness," in Dieter T. Hessel, ed., *Beyond Survival: Bread & Justice in Christian Perspective* (New York: Friendship Press, 1977), pp. 129-35.

8. Quoted from chapter 7, the NCCC study document, "Ethical Implications of Energy Production and Use."

9. Portions of this section are adopted from reports drafted by the author for 1971 and 1974 general assemblies of the United Presbyterian Church in the U.S.A. The author is indebted to Norman Faramelli and William Gibson for introducing him to the term, eco-justice.

10. Quoting Charles West, in a study paper, "Economic Justice within Environmental Limits," *Church and Society*, September-October 1976, p. 20.

11. The notion of obligation to, or respect for interests of future generations became a principle of ethical discourse only a decade ago, the earliest example being in Martin P. Golding, "Ethical Issues in Biological Engineering," *UCLA Law Review* 15 (1968), pp. 443-79

12. These ethical criteria are drawn from the "Report of the National Council of Churches Energy Ethics Consultation," October 12-14, 1977 (NCC Division of Church and Society, 1977), appendix C.

13. Vernon E. Jordan, "Energy Policy and Black People," address to Northern States Power Company Consumer/Utility Conference, Minneapolis, Minnesota, January 20, 1978.

Chapter 2: Energy and Society: Choosing a Future

1. Richard Lee and Irven DeVore, eds., *Man the Hunter: The First Intensive Survey of a Single, Crucial Stage of Human Development—Man's Once Universal Hunting Way of Life* (Chicago: Aldine Publishing Co., 1968).

2. Lewis Mumford, *The Myth of the Machine: Technics and Human Development* (New York: Harcourt, Brace & World, 1966).

3. Paul R. & Anne H. Ehrlich, *Population, Resources and Environment: Issues in Human Ecology* (San Francisco: W.H. Freeman, 1970).

4. Richard Gould, *Yiwara: Foragers of the Australian Desert: An Example* (New York: Charles Scribner's Sons, 1969). See especially chapter 5, "Desert Rituals and the Sacred Life."

Carl G. Jung, *Modern Man in Search of a Soul* (London: Routledge & Kegan Paul, 1933). See chapter, "Archaic Man," especially pp. 161-67.

5. Jung, *op. cit*, p. 6.

6. Harvey Cox, *The Secular City: Secularization & Urbanization in Theological Perspective* (New York: Macmillan, 1965). A celebration of its liberties and an invitation to its discipline. See particularly pp. 21-24.

Arend van Leeuwen, *Christianity in World History: The Meeting of the Faiths of East and West* (London: Edinburgh House Press, 1964). See especially chapter 2.

7. Lynn White, Jr., *Machina Ex Deo*, chapter 5, "The Historical Roots of the Ecological Crisis" (Cambridge, Mass.: M.I.T. Press, 1977), p. 8.

8. Jung, *op. cit.*, p. 8

9. Henry Adams, *The Education of Henry Adams: An Autobiography* (Boston: Houghton Mifflin, 1918). See especially "Dynamo & the Virgin," pp. 379-90 (quotations from pp. 380-85) and "Dynamo Theory of History," pp. 374-488 (quotations on Augustine and the Fall of Rome, pp. 480-81).

10. P.R. & A.H. Ehrlich, *op. cit.*, p. 10.

11. Leopold Kohr, *The Overdeveloped Nations: The Diseconomies of Scale* (New York: Schocken Books, 1978).

E.F. Schumacher, *Small Is Beautiful: Economics as if People Mattered* (New York: Harper Torchbook, 1973).

12. E.M. Forster, "The Machine Stops," pp. 261 ff. in *Of Men and Machines*, edited by Arthur O. Lewis, Jr. (New York: Dutton, 1963).

13. Reinhold Niebuhr, *Nature and Destiny of Man: A Christian Interpretation* (London: Nisbet, 1941). See especially "Sin as Sensuality," pp. 242 ff.

14. Ernest Becker, *The Denial of Death* (New York: Free Press, 1974), p. 284. (Also pp. 84 f., "The modern world, after all, has wanted to deny the person even his own body, even his emanation from his animal center; it has wanted to make him completely a depersonalized abstraction....").

15. John Snow, "Fear of Death and the Need to Accumulate," in *Ecology, Crisis and New Vision*, Richard E. Sherrell, ed. (Richmond, Va.: John Knox Press, 1971).

16. Dorothy Dinnerstein, *The Mermaid and the Minotaur: Sexual Arrangements and Human Malaise* (New York: Harper Colophon, 1976).

17. Jane Stembridge, a young poet active in Student Non-Violent Coordinating Committee in the civil rights movement of the sixties. As far as I know this poem has never been published.

18. Amory B. Lovins, *Soft Energy Paths: Toward a Durable Peace* (Cambridge, Mass.: Ballinger, 1977).

19. John E. Booty, "The Energy Crisis, Christianity and the Future," unpublished paper.

Chapter 3: Energy as a Moral and Religious Issue

1. I am using a somewhat artificial distinction between the moral, the political, and the religious. To be moral is to act in such a way that a certain conception of what is good or fulfilling is actualized. To be religious is to be grasped by that which is held to be ultimately significant, that which sustains and supports existence and meaning. Given a similar religious reality or faith, persons may still differ about what is moral. Thus, to say that the issue is moral means that, given some agreement on what is ultimately important, certain actions are judged to enhance and others are judged to undermine the ultimate values. To say that the issue is religious means that what is held to be ultimately significant is brought into question. Economic and political matters are moral matters concerning what is to be done institutionally in economic and political life in order to bring about the good life. They are economic or political matters insofar as they involve public policies or decisions within the framework of the economic and political institutions. And of course, they are religious matters insofar as they involve the *way of being* presupposed by the economic and political institutions.

2. Cf. A. L. Hammond, "Alcohol: A Brazilian Answer to the Energy Crisis." *Science,* February 11, 1977.

3. Consult *99 Ways to a Simple Lifestyle* (Washington, D.C.: Citizen's Energy Project, 1976).

4. I favor a moratorium on nuclear energy development since I do not think that we need nuclear energy, and since its use therefore involves what I consider unnecessary risks. I am well aware of the deep differences among the so-called experts in their judgments about its dangers and about the need for it.

5. See Ford Foundation (Energy Policy Project), *A Time to Choose*, pp. 440 ff., for some of the numbers which I use. Consult also "Energy Report from Chase," published monthly.

6. In spite of the loss of two-thirds of the heat value of coal, or gas, or oil in the production of electricity, I am informed that the use of heat pumps with an all-electrical home makes electricity as efficient as gas, or oil, or coal. I have not been able to check out the validity of this claim.

7. Cf. the preliminary report of the Ford Foundation Energy Policy Project, *Exploring Energy Choices* (Ford Foundation, 1974), section 7.

8. This could be less if very aggressive policies to reduce demand are followed. Cf. *Science*, April 1978, p. 145.

9. The use of thermal gradients may turn out to be feasible in fairly large projects by the year 2000.

10. R. Williams, ed., *The Energy Conservation Papers* (Cambridge, Mass.: Ballinger, 1975), pp. 219 ff.

11. *Ibid.*, and Proceedings of the 1976 Conference on *Capturing the Sun Through Bioconversion (CTSTB)*, pp. 145 ff., pp. 157 ff.

12. *CTSTB*, pp. 169 ff., 317 ff., 569 ff.

13. *CTSTB*, pp. 179 ff.

14. *CTSTB*, pp. 217 ff.

15. *CTSTB*, pp. 255 ff.

16. *CTSTB*, pp. 247 ff.

17. See appendix B for an estimate by C.G. Currin of Midland, Michigan, a participant in the Ghost Ranch seminar on energy, summer 1978.

Chapter 4: The Politics of Energy Policy

1. A standard and important source for understanding "the ecological perspective" is Barry Commoner's *The Closing Circle* (New York: Alfred A. Knopf, 1971).

2. The term is taken from the well-known book which aims at helping women develop a wholistic view of health and sexuality. The Boston Women's Health Book Collective, *Our Bodies, Ourselves* (New York: Simon and Schuster, 1972). The analogues between ecological critiques of our alienation from nature and feminist critiques of our alienation from body have been widely recognized and are usually integrated in discussion of eco-justice.

3. See for example Aldo Leopold, "The Conservation Ethic," in Robert Disch, ed., *The Ecological Conscience* (Englewood Cliffs, NJ.: Prentice-Hall, 1970).

4. The term is borrowed from Richard Bond, "Salvationists, Utilitarians, and Environmental Justice." Mimeographed essay, presented to The Group for Interdisciplinary Educational Research, Ramapo College Colloquium, 1975.

5. The phrase is a standard one in contemporary discussions of moral philosophy. Cf. John Rawls, *A Theory of Justice* (Cambridge, Mass.: Harvard University Press, 1971), p. 3 ff. When moral philos-

ophers like Rawls make this point, they generally mean to restrict the norm of justice to a specific arena of institutions. The biblical norm of justice does not permit such restriction.

6. An excellent theological analysis of this view of justice is found in Gustavo Gutierrez, *A Theology of Liberation* (Maryknoll, N.Y.: Orbis Books, 1973). Cf. especially part IV.

7. Cf. Matthew 25:31-46, Mark 1:21-28; 10:35-45 and parallels. For an excellent discussion of the contemporary significance of such texts, see Dorothee Sölle, *Political Theology* (Philadelphia: Fortress Press, 1974), chapters 3 through 8.

8. For clarification of the various meanings of justice, see Eugene Outka, *Agape* (New Haven, Conn.: Yale University Press), pp. 75-92.

9. *Exploring Energy Choices: A Preliminary Report*. Energy Policy Project of the Ford Foundation, 1974, pp. 23-28.

10. Robert Engler, *The Brotherhood of Oil* (New York: New American Library, 1977), chapter 4.

John Blair, *The Control of Oil* (New York: Pantheon, 1976), chapter 8.

11. Alternative ways of assessing governmental costs of nuclear power development can be seen by comparing Richard Munson, ed., *Countdown to a Nuclear Moratorium*, Environmental Action Foundation, 1976, and John Francis and Paul Albrecht, eds., *Facing Up to Nuclear Power* (Philadelphia: Westminster Press, 1976).

12. Engler, *op. cit.*, and Blair, *op. cit.*, pp. 371-400.

13. Blair, *op. cit.*, chapters 4, 7 and 8. Engler, *op. cit.*, pp. 139-98.

14. Alexander Cockburn and James Ridgeway, "Carter's Powerless Energy Policy," *The New York Review of Books*, May 24, 1977, pp. 31-36.

15. Robert Leckachman, "Carter's Energy Plan: Grade It C for Effort," *Christianity and Crisis*, vol. 37, no. 8, May 16, 1977, pp. 98-99.

16. For a summary of the complex compromise initially adopted on natural gas pricing, see *The New York Times*, Friday, November 10, 1978, pp. D1 and D14.

17. Those interested in studying the corporate positions may secure a booklet containing major advertisements run by the Mobil Corporation during the debate through P.O. Box NP, Mobil, 150 East 42nd Street, New York, N.Y. 10017.

18. *The New York Times*, April 17, 1977, p. E7, no. 6.

19. *Ibid.*, no. 8.

20. *Ibid.*, no. 6.

21. This way of distinguishing "needs" and luxuries is informed by Denis Goulet, *The Cruel Choice: A New Concept In the Theory of Development* (New York: Atheneum, 1973), pp. 240 f.

22. Campaign for Human Development, United States Catholic Conference, 1974: *Poverty in American Democracy*. This study is a refutation of the argument that it is the poor who benefit chiefly from governmental expenditures. See also Eugene Toland, et al., *World Justice and Peace: A Challenge to American Christians*. Church Research and Information Project, 1976.

23. Michael Lewis, *The Culture of Inequality* (Amherst, Mass.: University of Massachusetts Press, 1978), pp. 3-19.

24. Michael Harrington, *The Other America* (New York: Macmillan, 1970).

25. E. J. Kahn, "Who, What, Where, How Much, How Many," *The New Yorker* magazine, October 15, 1973. *The Civil Rights Digest*, spring 1974. U.S. Commission on Civil Rights, pp. 20 f.

26. For specification regarding the role played by these groups in advanced industrial society, cf. Barbara and John Ehrenreich, "The New Left and the Professional-Managerial Class," *Radical America*, vol. 11, no. 3, May-June 1977.

27. Leonard Silk, "Economic Scene: Energy Prices and Inflation," *The New York Times*, November 7, 1978, p. 68.

28. Bob Swierczek and David Tyler, "Energy and the Poor," in *Christianity and Crisis*, vol. 38, no. 15, October 16, 1978, pp. 242-246.

29. Cockburn and Ridgeway, *op. cit.*

30. Richard Grossman and Gail Daneker, "Jobs and Energy," Washington: Environmentalists for Full Employment, spring 1977.

31. Richard Grossman, "Energy and Employment," in *Christianity and Crisis*, vol. 28, no. 15, October 16, 1978, p. 247.

32. See the chapter by Douglas Still in this volume.

33. For specification of some United States aid policies related to energy which can help the poor, see Swierczek and Tyler, *op. cit.*

Chapter 5: Ways to Influence Energy Systems

1. Excerpts from remarks before the Senate Subcommittee on Intergovernmental Relations, Committee on Government Operations, March 4, 1969.

2. Richard Morgan and Sandra Jerabek, "How to Challenge Your Electric Utility," *Environmental Action Foundation* booklet, March 1974, p. 12.

3. Ivan Illich, *Tools of Conviviality*. Amory B. Lovins, *Soft Energy Paths: Toward a Durable Peace* (Cambridge, Mass.: Ballinger, 1977).

4. Information from ERDA, vol. 3, no. 21, May 27, 1977, pp. 77-78.

5. Task Force Against Nuclear Pollution, Inc., 153 E Street, SE, Washington, D.C. 20003.

Chapter 6: Exodus from Nuclear Bondage

1. Alvin M. Weinberg made this case in "Social Institutions and Nuclear Energy," *Science*, vol. 177, July 7, 1972.

2. For discussion of this relationship, see Amory B. Lovins and John H. Price, *Non-Nuclear Futures* (Cambridge, Mass.: Ballinger, 1975), ch. 2; Lovins, "Energy Strategy: The Road Not Taken?" *Foreign Affairs*, October 1976; Lovins, *Soft Energy Paths* (Cambridge, Mass: Ballinger, 1977), and Mark Reader, ed., *Energy: The Human Dimension* (Tempe, Arizona: Arizona State University Center for Environment Studies, 1977).

3. For a statement of the Ford administration-Carter positions on the nuclear energy question on the eve of the 1976 elections, see the articles by candidate Jimmy Carter and Ford administration spokesman, Fred C. Iklé, in the October 1976 issue of the *Bulletin of the Atomic Scientists*.

4. Occupation of the proposed site of the Seabrook, N.H. reactor by some 2,000 protesters began on April 30, 1976, a week after the Mobilization for Survival, an anti-nuclear weapons and anti-nuclear reactor coalition was formed in Philadelphia. Mass demonstrations at nuclear plant sites had been experienced in Whyl, West Germany as early as February 1975, and have continued intermittently in Germany and France ever since.

5. National Council of Churches of Christ in the U.S.A., "The Plutonium Economy: A Statement of Concern" (September 1975).

6. William Epstein, "Why States Go—and Don't Go—Nuclear," Nuclear Proliferation: Prospects, Problems and Proposals issue of *The Annals of the American Academy of Political and Social Science*, March 1977, pp. 16-28.

7. Denis Hayes, "Nuclear Power: The Fifth Horseman," *The Humanist*, September-October 1976, p. 26.

8. Should United States energy demands continue to increase without interruption until 1985, Lovins estimates the domestic nuclear fuel cycle will require "over 100 new uranium mines, a new enrichment plant, some 40 fuel fabrication plants, three fuel reprocessing plants...the year 2000 finds us with 450 to 800 reactors (including perhaps 80 fast breeders, each loaded with 2.5 metric tons of plutonium)...." Lovins, "Energy Strategy," *op. cit.*

9. Mason Willrich, "Terrorists Keep Out!" *Bulletin of the Atomic Scientists*, vol. XXXI, no. 5, May 1975, pp. 12-16.

10. As early as 1958, my mentor at the University of Michigan, James H. Meisel, was suggesting that if America ever "went fascist" it would happen because people had learned how to think like generals and forgotten how to think like noncombatants.

11. Garrett Hardin, "Living with the Faustian Bargain," *Bulletin of the Atomic Scientists*, vol. XXXII, no. 9, p. 25.

12. Mumford's work is in two volumes. Volume One, *The Myth of the Machine: Technics and Human Development* (New York: Harcourt and Brace), was published in 1967, and Volume Two, *The Myth of the Machine: Pentagon of Power* (New York: Harcourt and Brace), made its appearance in book form in 1970.

13. Among the most far-reaching pieces of federal domestic legislation was the National Environmental Policy Act (1969). The Stockholm declaration did not go far enough for many because of its acceptance of entrenched economic and national interests.

14. For full citation, see Reader, "Political Culture in the Nuclear Age," *Peace and Change*, *op. cit.*

15. Sidney Lens, "The Doomsday Strategy," *The Progressive*, vol. 40, no. 2, February 1976, pp. 12-35.

16. *Ibid.*, p. 34.

17. S. Burnham, ed., *The Threat to Licensed Nuclear Facilities*, The Mitre Corporation, MTR-7022, McLean, Virginia, September 1975. This report has been discussed in greater detail by David Dinsmore Comey, "The Perfect Trojan Horse," *Bulletin of the Atomic Scientists*, June 1976, pp. 33-34.

18. The Washington-based Citizen's Energy Project has recently released a monograph of nuclear-related civil liberties violations in the United States.

BIBLIOGRAPHY

Abrecht, Paul and Francis, John, eds. *Facing Up to Nuclear Power.* Philadelphia, Pa: Westminster Press, 1976.

Adams, Henry. *The Education of Henry Adams—An Autobiography.* 1918. Reprint. Dunwoody, Ga: Norman S. Berg, Pub., 1976.

Adelman, Morris A., et al. *No Time to Confuse.* San Francisco: Institute for Contemporary Studies, 1975.

Barnet, Richard J. and Muller, Ronald E. *Global Reach—The Power of the Multinational Corporations.* New York: Simon & Schuster, 1975.

Battelle Pacific Northwest Laboratories. "Toward a Methodology for Conducting Social Life Indicators." Prepared for the U.S. Energy Research & Development Administration under contract at (45.1): 1830 BNWL-2084 RA P-2 US-11, July 1976.

Becker, Ernest. *The Denial of Death.* New York: Free Press, 1973.

Berry, Wendell. *The Unsettling of America: Culture and Agriculture* San Francisco: Sierra Club Press, 1977.

Blair, John M. *The Control of Oil.* New York: Pantheon, 1977.

Bohi, Douglas R. and Russell, Milton. *U.S. Energy Policy: Alternatives for Security.* (Resources for the Future) Baltimore: Johns Hopkins, 1975.

Bond, Richard. "Salvationists, Utilitarians, and Environmental Justice." Mimeographed essay. Ramapo College of New Jersey, Mahway, NJ: Ramapo College Colloquium, The Group for Interdisciplinary Educational Research, 1975.

Booty, John E. "The Energy Crisis, Christianity and the Future." Unpublished paper. Cambridge, Mass: Episcopal Divinity School.

The Boston Women's Health Collective. *Our Bodies, Ourselves: A Book By and For Women.* New York: Simon & Schuster, 1972.

Boulding, Kenneth E. *The Meaning of the Twentieth Century: The Great Transition.* New York: Harper and Row, 1964.

Brookhaven National Laboratories. "Energy Needs, Uses and Resources in Developing Countries." Prepared for U.S. Agency for International Development. PASA No. ERDA/TAB 995-18-78, March 1978.

Brueggemann, Walter. *The Land—Place as Gift, Promise and Challenge in Biblical Faith.* Philadelphia: Fortress Press, 1977.

Budnitz, Robert J. and Holdren, John P. "Social and Environmental Costs of Energy Systems," *Annual Review of Energy,* Jack M. Hollander, et al., eds. Vol. I. Palo Alto, Calif: Annual Reviews Inc., 1976.

Bupp, Irvin C. and Derian, Claude. *Light Water: How the Nuclear Dream Dissolved.* New York: Basic Books, 1978.

Burnham, S., ed. *The Threat to Licensed Nuclear Facilities.* MTR-7022. McLean, Va: The Mitre Corporation, September 1975.

Campaign for Human Development. United States Catholic Conference. *Poverty in American Democracy: A Study of Social Power.* Washington: United States Catholic Conference, 1974.

Caudill, Harry. *The Watches of the Night.* Boston: Little, Brown & Co., 1976.

"The Churches and the Nuclear Debate," *Anticipation* 24 (1977).

Clark, Wilson. *Energy for Survival.* Garden City, NY: Anchor Books, 1975.

Cockburn, Alexander and Ridgeway, James. "Carter's Powerless Energy Policy," *The New York Review of Books* (May 26, 1977): 31-36. A review of the national energy plan from the Executive Office of the President.

Comey, David Dinsmore. "The Perfect Trojan Horse," *Bulletin of Atomic Scientists* 32 (June 1976): 33-34.

Commoner, Barry. *The Poverty of Power—Energy and the Economic Crisis*. New York: Alfred A. Knopf, 1976.

————. *The Closing Circle*. New York: Alfred A. Knopf, 1971.

Cortese, Charles F. and Jones, Bernie. "Energy Boomtown: A Social Impact Model and Annotated Bibliography," in "Study of Nuclear and Alternative Energy Systems," Supporting Paper 5: *Sociopolitical Effects of Energy Use and Policy*. Edited by Charles T. Unseld, et al. Washington: National Academy of Sciences, 1979.

Cox, Harvey. *The Secular City—Secularization and Urbanization in Theological Perspective*. New York: Macmillan, 1965.

Daly, Herman E. "Energy Demand Forecasting: Prediction or Planning?" *American Institute of Planners Journal* (January 1976): 12.

————. *Toward a Steady-State Economy*. San Francisco: W. H. Freeman & Co., 1973.

Deolalikar, Anil B. "Gandhian Economics: What Is It? and How Relevant Is It for Today?" Unpublished paper. Cambridge, Mass: Harvard University Center of Population Studies.

Dinnerstein, Dorothy. *The Mermaid and the Minotaur—Sexual Arrangements and Human Malaise*. New York: Harper and Row, 1976.

Disch, Robert, ed. *Ecological Conscience: Values for Survival*. (A Spectrum Book). Englewood Cliffs, NJ: Prentice-Hall, 1970.

"Don't Leave It All to the Experts: Citizens Role in Environmental Decision Making." Washington, DC: U.S. Environmental Protection Agency, Office of Public Affairs.

Eccli, Eugene, ed. *Low-Cost, Energy-Efficient Shelter*. Emmaus, Pa: Rodale Press, 1976.

Ehrenreich, Barbara and John. "The New Left and the Professional-Managerial Class," *Radical America* 11, no. 3 (May-June 1977).

Ehrlich, Paul R. and Ehrlich, Anne H. *Population, Resources and Environment—Issues in Human Ecology*. 2nd ed. San Francisco: W. H. Freeman & Co., 1972.

"Energy for a Just, Sustainable Society," *Anticipation* 23 (1976).

Energy Policy Project of the Ford Foundation. Energy Report. Philadelphia, Pa: Lippincott, 1975.

Energy Reports from Chase. New York: Chase Manhattan Bank.

Engler, Robert. *The Brotherhood of Oil: Energy Policy and the Public Interest.* New York: New American Library, 1977.

Epstein, William. "Why States Go—and Don't Go—Nuclear," *The Annals of the American Academy of Political and Social Science* 430 (1977): 16-28.

Exploring Energy Choices: A Preliminary Report. Energy Policy Project of the Ford Foundation. New York: The Ford Foundation, 1974.

Finnerty, Adam. *No More Plastic Jesus—Global Justice and Christian Life Style.* Maryknoll, NY: Orbis Books, 1977.

Ford, D.F., et al. *The Nuclear Fuel Cycle—A Survey of the Public Health, Environmental and National Security Effects of Nuclear Power.* Union of Concerned Scientists, Friends of the Earth Energy Paper No. 2. San Francisco: Friends of the Earth, 1974.

Ford Foundation (Energy Policy Project). *A Time to Choose: America's Energy Future.* Cambridge, Mass: Ballinger, 1974.

Forster, E.M. "The Machine Stops," in *Of Men and Machines.* Edited by Arthur O. Lewis. New York: Dutton, 1963.

Fuller, John G. *We Almost Lost Detroit.* New York: Dist. by T.Y. Crowell, Reader's Digest Press, 1975.

Gibson, William E. "The Lifestyle of Christian Faithfulness," in *Beyond Survival: Bread and Justice in Christian Perspective.* Edited by Dieter T. Hessel. New York: Friendship Press, 1977.

Glesk, Martin and Paradise, Scott. "Fuel, Food and Faith," in *Beyond Survival: Bread and Justice in Christian Perspective.* Edited by Dieter T. Hessel. New York: Friendship Press, 1977.

Gold, Raymond L. "Toward Social Policy on Regionalizing Energy Production and Consumption." Unpublished paper. Missoula, Mont: University of Montana, Institute for Social Research, June 1977.

Golding, Martin P. "Ethical Issues in Biological Engineering," *UCLA Law Review* 15 (1968): 443-79.

Goldsmith, Edward and Ecologist Editors. *Blueprint for Survival.* Boston: Houghton Mifflin, 1972.

Gould, Richard. *Yiwara: Foragers of the Australian Desert.* New York: Charles Scribner's Sons, 1969.

Goulet, Denis. *The Cruel Choice: A New Concept in the Theory of Development.* New York: Atheneum, 1971.

Grier, Eunice S. *Colder...Darker: The Energy Crisis and Low-Income Americans.* Prepared by the Washington Center for Metropolitan Studies. Washington: Community Services Administration, June 1977.

Grossman, Richard L. "Energy and Employment," *Christianity and Crisis* 28, no. 15 (October 16, 1978): 247-49.

Grossman, Richard and Daneker, Gail. "Jobs and Energy." Washington, DC: Environmentalists for Full Employment, spring 1977.

Gutierrez, Gustavo. *A Theology of Liberation.* Translated by Caridad Inda and John Eagleson. Maryknoll, NY: Orbis Books, 1972.

Halacy, D.S. Jr. *The Coming Age of Solar Energy.* New York: Avon Press, 1975.

Hammond, A. L. "Alcohol: A Brazilian Answer to the Energy Crisis," *Science* 195 (1977): 564-6.

Hannon, Bruce M. "Energy and Labor Demand in the Conserver Society." Unpublished paper. Urbana, Ill: University of Illinois at Urbana-Champaign, Energy Research Group, Center for Advanced Computation, July 1976.

Hardin, Garrett. "Living with the Faustian Bargain," *Bulletin of Atomic Scientists* 32, no. 9 (1976): 25-29.

Harrington, Michael. *The Other America: Poverty in the United States.* Rev. ed. New York: Macmillan, 1970.

Hayes, Denis. "Nuclear Power: The Fifth Horseman," *The Humanist* 36 (September/October 1976): 26-33.

_____. *Energy: The Case for Conservation.* Worldwatch Paper 4. Washington: Worldwatch Institute, 1976.

_____. *Energy: The Solar Prospect.* Worldwatch Paper 11. Washington: Worldwatch Institute, 1977.

_____. *Rays of Hope.* New York: W. W. Norton & Co., Inc., 1977.

Henderson, Hazel. "Economics: A Paradigm Shift Is in Progress," *Solar Age* (August 1978): 18-21.

Hessel, Dieter T. *A Social Action Primer*. Philadelphia: Westminster, 1972.

Illich, Ivan. *Tools for Conviviality*. New York: Harper and Row, 1973.

Jewett, Robert and Laurence, John Shelton. *The American Monomyth*. Garden City, NY: Doubleday, 1977.

Jonas, Hans. "Technology and Responsibility: Reflections on the New Tasks of Ethics," *Social Research* 40 (1973): 31-54.

Jordan, Vernon E. "Energy Policy and Black People." Address to Northern States Power Company Consumer Utility Conference, Minneapolis, Minn. January 20, 1978. New York: National Urban League.

Jung, Carl G. *Modern Man in Search of a Soul*. 1933. Reprint. New York: Harcourt Brace Jovanovich, 1955.

Kahn, Ely Jacques. "Who, What, Where, How Much, How Many," *The New Yorker* 49 (October 15, 1973): 105-8.

Kahn, Herman. *The Next Two Hundred Years*. New ed. New York: Morrow, 1976.

Kohr, Leopold. *The Overdeveloped Nations—The Diseconomies of Scale*. New York: Schocken, 1978.

LaPorte, Todd R. "Nuclear Waste: Increasing Scale and Sociopolitical Impacts," *Science* 201 (1978): 22-8.

Leckachman, Robert. "Carter's Energy Plan: Grade It C for Effort," *Christianity and Crisis* 37, no. 8 (May 16, 1977): 98-99.

Leckie, Jim, ed., et al. *Other Homes and Garbage*. San Francisco: Sierra Club Books, 1975.

Lee, Richard and Devore, Irven, eds. *Man the Hunter: The First Intensive Survey of a Single, Crucial Stage of Human Development—Man's Once Universal Hunting Way of Life*. Chicago: Aldine Publishing Co., 1968.

Lens, Sidney, "The Doomsday Strategy," *The Progressive* 40, no. 2 (1976): 12-35.

Leopold, Aldo. "The Conservation Ethic," *The Ecological Conscience: Values for Survival.* Edited by Robert Disch. Englewood Cliffs, NJ: Prentice-Hall, 1970.

Lewis, Michael. *The Culture of Inequality.* Amherst, Mass: University of Massachusetts, 1978.

Louviere, Vernon. "Energy: Here Today, Gone Tomorrow?" *Nation's Business* 66 (1978): 28-34.

Lovins, Amory B. "The Soft Energy Path," *The Center Magazine* 11, no. 5 (September-October 1978): 32 ff.

_____. "Energy Strategy: The Road Not Taken?" *Foreign Affairs* 55 (1976): 65-96.

_____. *Soft Energy Paths, Toward a Durable Peace.* Cambridge, Mass: Ballinger, 1977.

_____. *World Energy Strategies.* San Francisco: Friends of the Earth. Co-publisher: Cambridge, Mass: Ballinger, 1975.

Lovins, Amory B. and Price, John. *Non-Nuclear Futures: The Case for Ethical Energy Strategy.* (The Energy Paper Series.) San Francisco: Friends of the Earth. Co-publisher: Cambridge, Mass: Ballinger, 1975.

Meadows, Donella H., et al. 1972. *The Limits to Growth—A Report for the Club of Rome's Project on the Predicament of Mankind.* 2nd ed. New York: Universe, 1974.

Metcalf, Lee L. and Reinemer, Victor. *Overcharge.* New York: David McKay Co., Inc., 1967.

Mitchell, John G. and Stallings, Constance, eds. *Ecotactics: The Sierra Club Handbook for Environmental Activists.* Los Angeles: S. & S. Enterprises, 1970.

Morgan, Richard and Jerabek, Sandra. *How to Challenge Your Local Electric Utility.* Booklet. Washington: Environmental Action Foundation, 1974.

Mumford, Lewis. *The Myth of the Machine.* 2 vols. 1967. Vol. I, *Technics and Human Development.* (Reprint of 1967 ed.) Vol. II, *Pentagon of Power.* (Reprint of 1970 ed.) New York: Harcourt Brace Jovanovich, Inc., 1971 and 1974.

Munson, Richard, ed. *Countdown to a Nuclear Moratorium.* Washington: Environmental Action Foundation, 1976.

Nader, Ralph and Abbotts, John. *The Menace of Atomic Energy.* New York: Norton, 1977.

National Council of Churches of Christ. *National Church Panel on Strip Mining and the Energy Crisis.* New York: Interfaith Center on Corporate Responsibility and the Commission on Religion in Appalachia (NCC), 1974.

_____. "The Plutonium Economy: A Statement of Concern." New York: National Council of Churches, September 1975.

National Science Teachers Association. *Energy Environment Source Book.* Washington: National Science Teachers Association, 1975.

Niebuhr, Reinhold. *Nature and Destiny of Man: A Christian Interpretation.* 1941. Reprint. 2 vol. *Human Nature* and *Human Destiny.* New York: Scribner, 1949.

1977 Energy and Research Directory. New ed. Ann Arbor, Mich: Ann Arbor Science Pubs., 1977.

Odum, Howard T. *Environment Power and Society.* New York: Wiley-Interscience, 1971.

Outka, Gene. *Agape: An Ethical Analysis.* (Publications in Religion Series, No. 17) New Haven, Conn: Yale University Press, 1972. Paper 1977.

Pfeiffer, John. *The Emergence of Man.* 1969. 2nd ed. New York: Harper & Row, 1972.

The Proceedings of the 1976 Conference on Capturing the Sun Through Bioconversion. Washington: Bioenergy Council, 1976.

Rawls, John. *A Theory of Justice.* Cambridge, Mass: Harvard University Press, 1971.

Reader, Mark, ed. *Energy: The Human Dimension.* Research Paper No. 5. Tempe, Ariz: Arizona State University, Center for Environmental Studies, 1977.

Ryan, Charles. "The Choices in the Next Energy and Social Revolution." Mitchell Prize Winning Essay 1977. Hanover, NH: Dartmouth College, Thayer School of Engineering.

Sahlins, Marshall. *Stone Age Economics.* Chicago: Aldine-Atherton, Inc., 1972.

Schipper, Lee. *Explaining Energy: A Manual of Non-Style for the Energy Outsider Who Wants In.* Berkeley, Calif: University of California, 1975.

Schumacher, E.F. *Small Is Beautiful: Economics as if People Mattered.* New York: Harper & Row, 1973.

Scully, Dan, et al. *The Fuel Savers: A Kit of Solar Ideas for Existing Homes.* Harrisville, NH: Total Environmental Action, 1978.

Shinn, Roger L. "Faith, Science, Ideology and the Nuclear Decision," *Christianity and Crisis* 39, no. 1 (1979): 3-8.

Silk, Leonard. "Economic Scene, Energy Prices and Inflation," *The New York Times* (Nov. 7, 1978): 68.

Snow, John. "Fear of Death and the Need to Accumulate," in *Ecology, Crisis and New Vision.* Edited by Richard E. Sherrell. Richmond [Atlanta]: John Knox Press, 1971.

Sölle, Dorothee. *Political Theology.* Translated from the German by John Shelley. Philadelphia: Fortress Press, 1974.

Steinhart, Carol and Steinhart, John. *The Fires of Culture: Energy Yesterday and Tomorrow.* North Scituate, Mass: Duxbury, 1974.

Stoner, Carol Hupping, ed. *Goodbye to the Flush Toilet.* Emmaus, Pa: Rodale Press, 1977.

Swierczek, Bob and Tyler, David. "Energy and the Poor," *Christianity and Crisis* 38, no. 15 (1978): 242-246.

Total Environmental Action. *The Energy Efficient Church.* New York: Pilgrim Press, Spring 1979.

U.S. Dept. of Energy. Office of Consumer Affairs. *The Great Adventure.* (Report on Regional Public Hearings on Solar Energy.) October 1978. HCP/U6354-01. Springfield, Va: National Technical Information Service (NTIS).

Van Dresser, Peter. *A Landscape for Humans—A Case Study of the Potentials for Ecologically Guided Development in an Upland Region.* Albuquerque, NM: Biotechnic Press, 1972. Subsequently published *Development on a Human Scale: Potentials for Ecologically Guided Growth in Northern New Mexico.* New York: Praeger, 1973.

Van Leeuwen, Arend T. *Christianity in World History—The Meeting of the Faiths of East and West.* 1964. New York: Scribner, 1966.

Weinberg, Alvin M. "Social Institutions and Nuclear Energy," *Science* 177 (July 7, 1972): 27-34.

West, Charles. "Economic Justice within Environmental Limits," *Church and Society* 67, no. 1 (1976): 20.

White, Lynn, Jr. *Dynamo and Virgin Reconsidered: Machina Ex Deo.* Cambridge, Mass: M.I.T. Press, 1971.

Williams, Robert, ed. *The Energy Conservation Papers.* (Energy Policy Project of the Ford Foundation) Cambridge, Mass: Ballinger, 1975.

Willrich, Mason. "Terrorists Keep Out! The Problem of Safe-Guarding Nuclear Materials," *Bulletin of Atomic Scientists* 31, no. 5 (1975): 12-16.

Winner, Langdon. *Autonomous Technology—Technics-out-of-Control as a Theme for Political Thought.* Cambridge, Mass: M.I.T. Press, 1977.

Woodwell, George M. "The Carbon Dioxide Question," *Scientific American* 238, no. 12 (1978): 34-43.

World Council of Churches. Church and Society. *Faith, Science and the Future.* Preparatory Readings for World Conference, Massachusetts Institute of Technology (M.I.T.), Cambridge, Massachusetts, July 14-24, 1979. Geneva, Switzerland: World Council of Churches, 1978.

A Select List of Organizations and Resources

The American Petroleum Institute (and related energy producer groups) have specific public policy interests that are described in "Policy for Energy and Energy for Policy," *The Fires of Culture* by Carol and John Steinhart (Duxbury Press, 1974), or contact The American Petroleum Institute, 1808 K Street N.W., Washington, D.C.

Bishops' Committee for Human Values (National Conference of Catholic Bishops), 1312 Massachusetts Ave. N.W., Washington, D.C. 20005.

Chase Manhattan Bank "Energy Reports." Department of Energy Economics, 1 Chase Manhattan Plaza, 10th Floor, New York, N.Y. 10005.

Citizen's Energy Project, 1110 6 Street N.W., Washington, D.C. 20001. "Life Style Index '77" and "Personal Energy Accounting System," "99 Ways to a Simple Lifestyle."

Commission on Religion in Appalachia (CORA), 864 Weisgarber Road N.W., Knoxville, Tenn. 37919.

Energy Research Group Center for Advanced Computation, University of Illinois at Urbana-Champaign, Urbana, Ill. 61801.

Interfaith Center on Corporate Responsibility, Room 566, 475 Riverside Drive, New York, N.Y. 10027.

166

Interfaith Coalition on Energy, 110 Maryland Avenue N.E., Washington, D.C. 20002.

Joint Strategy and Action Committee (JSAC), Room 1700 A, 475 Riverside Drive, New York, N.Y. 10027.

League of Women Voters, 730 M Street N.W., Washington, D.C. "Final Report for Energy Conservation, Technology, Education Project." Project reports on Phoenix, Az; Northfield, Mn; West Hartford, Ct; Wake County (Raleigh), N.C. "Final Report for Energy Education Outreach Program." Project reports from fifty states, District of Columbia, Puerto Rico, and the Virgin Islands. Both reports available from National Technical Information Service (NTIS), Department of Energy Conservation and Solar Conservation, 5285 Port Royale Road, Springfield, Va. 22161.

National Council of Churches of Christ, Room 572, 475 Riverside Drive, New York, N.Y. 10027. Educational materials available are:

1. "The Social Costs of Energy Choices," *Christianity and Crisis* (October 16, 1978). $.90 per copy
2. "Energy Oratorio," a worship service by Elizabeth Dodson Gray. $1.50 per copy
3. "Church Energy Kit." $.90 plus postage
4. "The Plutonium Economy." $.50 per copy
5. "Energy and Ethics: The Ethical Implications of Energy Production and Use." $1.00 per copy
6. "Energy and the New Poverty," Katherine D. Seelman with David Dodson Gray, ed. $1.00 per copy
7. "The Energy Suppliers: A Guide to America's Oil, Natural Gas, Coal and Electric Utility Industries," Carter Henderson. $1.00 per copy

Shell Oil Company, P.O. Box 10, Houston, Tex. 77001. "The Energy Book—Where Will We Get the Fuels for Our Future," "National Energy Outlook 1980-1990," and "The Story of Petroleum and Solar Energy."

Sierra Club, 530 Busch, San Francisco, Calif.

Synod of the Northeast (United Presbyterian Church U.S.A.). Ministries Agency. 3041 Genesee Street, Syracuse, N.Y. 13224. "Energy Conservation Report."

Total Environmental Action, Church Hill, Harrisville, N.H. 03450.

United Plainsmen, Dunn Center, N. Dak. 58626.

U.S. Community Services Administration, 1200 19th Street N.W., Washington, D.C. 20506. "Save Energy! Save Money!" and "A Community Planning Guide to Weatherization."

Women for Peace, 201 Massachusetts Avenue, N.E., No. 102A, Washington, D.C. 20002 .

World Council of Churches, Department of Church and Society, 150 Route de Ferney, 1211 Geneva 20, Switzerland. "Energy for My Neighbor" program offers up-to-date information on energy requirements of different countries and contact with appropriate energy development projects in Africa, Asia, and Latin America.

Worldwatch Institute, 1776 Massachusetts Avenue N.W., Washington, D.C. 20036.

Magazines

Anticipation: Christian Social Thought in a Future Perspective. World Council of Churches, Church and Society, 150 Route de Ferney, 1211 Geneva 20, Switzerland.

Bulletin of Atomic Scientists. Kent Chemical Laboratory, 1020-24 E. 58 Street, Chicago, Ill. 60637.

The Civil Rights Digest. U.S. Commission on Human Rights, 1121 Vermont Avenue, Washington, D.C. 20425.

Critical Mass. Citizen's Movement for Safe and Efficient Energy, P.O. Box 1538, Washington, D.C. 20013.

The Element: A Journal of World Resources. Public Resource Center, 1747 Connecticut Avenue, N.W., Washington, D.C. 20009.

The Energy Consumer. Department of Energy, Office of Consumer Affairs, Room 8G031, Washington, D.C. 20585.

Environmental Action. Environmental Action Inc., Suite 731, 1346 Connecticut Avenue, N.W., Washington, D.C. 20036.

Just Economics. The Movement for Economic Justice, 1735 T Street N.W., Washington, D.C. 20009.

Not Man Apart. Friends of the Earth, 124 Spear Street, San Francisco, Calif. 94105.

People and Energy. Institute for Ecological Policies, 1413 K Street N.W., Washington, D.C. 20005.

The Power Line. Environmental Action Foundation, 724 Dupont Circle Building, Washington, D.C. 20036.

Sojourners. Peoples Christian Coalition, 1309 L Street, N.W., Washington, D.C. 20005.

Audio-Visual Sources

Arizona State University Center for Environmental Studies. Tempe, Ariz. "Energy: The Human Dimension," sound-slide presentation on values and alternatives.

Arthur Barr Productions. P.O. Box 7-C, Pasadena, Calif. 91104. "A Thousand Suns." (film)

Bullfrog Films. Oley, Pa. 19547. Catalogue features appropriate technology.

Center for Renewable Resources. 1028 Connecticut Avenue, N.W., Washington, D.C. 20036. Order "Solar Energy Bibliography for Elementary, Secondary, and College Students (Annotated)," $2.50. General source for films, slides, video cassettes, and reading materal on renewable energy resources.

Danamar Film. 275 Kilby, Los Alamos, N. Mex. 87544. "Building a Solar Greenhouse." (film)

Encyclopedia Britannica Education Corp. 425 N. Michigan Avenue, Chicago, Ill. 60611. "Energy from the Sun." (film)

Envision Corporation Film Producers. 51 Sleeper Street, Boston, Mass. 02210. "Energy: Crisis and Challenge." (film)

Green Mountain Post Films. P.O. Box 177, Montague, Mass. 01351. Source on nuclear energy; coal.

Lumen Associates. 144 W. 27th Street, New York, N.Y. 10001. Video tapes on appropriate technology and the Third World. "Tchuba Wind Energy Summary." (Video Tape)

Lumen-Bel Inc. 303 W. 11th Street, New York, N.Y. 10014. "A Place to Live." (film) Building a house using passive solar techniques.

National Geographic Educational. 17th and M Streets N.W., Washington, D.C. 20036. "Energy: The Problems and the Future." (film)

U.S. Department of Energy Film Library. Box 62, Oak Ridge, Tenn. 37830.

NOTE: Catalogues of resources may be requested from these sources.